MR. LINCOLN SPEAKS AT GETTYSBURG

MR. LINCOLN SPEAKS AT GETTYSBURG

by

Mary Kay Phelan

W · W · NORTON & COMPANY · INC · *New York*

Photo Credits

Facsimiles of the five versions of the Gettysburg Address are from *Long Remembered,* used with the courtesy of The Library of Congress.

First Edition

Library of Congress Catalog Card No. 66-10791

Published simultaneously in Canada by George J. McLeod Limited, Toronto

Printed in the United States of America

1 2 3 4 5 6 7 8 9 0

To my favorite critics—
Marty, Dick, and Jerry

Contents

List of Illustrations

Acknowledgments

The author gratefully acknowledges the use of photographs from the Library of Congress, the National Park Service, the National Archives, the White House Collection, and the Lane Studio in Gettysburg, Pennsylvania. Special thanks are due to Miss Josephine Cobb, Specialist in Iconography at the National Archives, for her assistance in locating the various photographs.

The Honorable Fred Schwengel, President of the United States Capitol Historical Society, provided enthusiasm and encouragement for this manuscript. His discerning comments were most helpful in both the research and editing.

Introduction

To make history come alive in her writing has long been the aspiration of the author of this book. She firmly believes that by an enriched understanding of our American past the people of today's complex world can prepare to build a better future.

It is fortunate that each year millions read, and hundreds of thousands of students throughout this nation and the world memorize, the Gettysburg Address. This address will become even more meaningful to the readers of Mary Kay Phelan's book, *Mr. Lincoln Speaks At Gettysburg*; and the fervor and feeling of these words will become more intense when the address is recited from memory. What has long been proclaimed as one of the world's finest pieces of literature needs a better understanding. Too often the immortal words are repeated by rote with little, if any, realization of what Mr. Lincoln had on his mind and in his heart on that faraway day in November of 1863. The author has sifted out the little details, as well as the big ones, that are needed for a more thorough understanding of this great moment in history and its impact.

The events leading up to the delivery of the address at Gettysburg, the press reports, and the reaction of the country are accurately described here in language and style which are both pleasurable and informative. The tracing of the present existing copies of the Gettysburg Address manuscripts is interesting and will be appreciated by students of Lincoln. Mrs. Phelan has attempted with success to make Lincoln's address, to many students the greatest of all his speeches, become a vivid, lasting memory for the readers of today.

This is another of the author's books that will add to a better understanding and appreciation of our heritage. It will and should be read by many. It should be placed on the library shelves for those who may not be able to acquire a book of their own.

The Hon. Fred B. Schwengel
President, the United States Capitol Historical Society, Wash., D.C.

MR. LINCOLN
SPEAKS AT GETTYSBURG

National Park Service

Matthew Brady, the photographer of Civil War fame, took this first picture of the White House during Mr. Lincoln's administration.

ONE

Two Invitations

IT was late—really, quite late—on this mid-October night in 1863. An uneasy calm seemed to have settled over the city of Washington. The stately White House at 1600 Pennsylvania Avenue was wreathed in shadows, with the only light in the mansion coming from the east wing of the second floor—"the business wing," Mr. Lincoln called it.

Glass-globed gas jets suspended from the ceiling gave off a flickering glow in the rectangular room which the President used as his office. The furnishings were sparse: a large oak table for cabinet meetings, a few straight-backed chairs, two hair-covered sofas. No one had bothered much about pictures. Above the marble-mantled fireplace hung an engraving of President Jackson, now discolored by time. Someone had put up a photograph of the English liberal, John Bright. And there were various military maps in wooden frames, arranged in no particular sequence.

A tall pigeonhole desk stood against the south wall. The openings were labeled with the names of cabinet members and generals, and the President used the desk primarily for filing memorandums to these persons. He preferred to work at the long table between the two windows which overlooked the Potomac River. Now, seated in his favorite armchair beside the table, Mr. Lincoln was studying the huge stack of papers which one of his secretaries, John Nicolay, had left for him.

There had been a constant stream of callers all day: congressmen, senators, soldiers, people seeking favors of every description. Then after dinner the mischievous ten-year-old Tad had begged for a gallop with his father, "Please, please, Papa-Day, just a short ride!"

Ever since Tad's brother, Willie, had died the previous year, Mr. Lincoln had been his youngest son's dearest companion. Never able to deny any request that Tad made, the father had hoisted the youngster up on his broad shoulders and set off on the nightly trot up and down the corridor of their private apartments in the west wing.

The President knew that most people thought he was too indulgent with the boy. But Tad was such a lovable child. The cleft palate which gave him a slight lisp endeared him even more to the adoring father.

The romp and tucking in of the lad had consumed a longer time than he had expected. Numerous problems had to be solved; there were always problems, it seemed. And he spent some time at one of the large windows, trying to think out solutions. He always liked that view; somehow, he could think better when he watched the river. It was with some reluctance that he returned to the stack of papers.

Now, a printed invitation caught the President's eye. It was an announcement of dedication ceremonies at the newly formed National Cemetery on November 19, 1863, in Gettysburg, Pennsylvania. The invitation itself was exactly like hundreds of other circulars which had been mailed to senators, congressmen, members of the cabinet, governors of the northern states, Army and Navy "brass," and dignitaries throughout the country.

Although he had never been in Gettysburg, President Lincoln felt he knew the place intimately. He had followed every move which General Meade made during those perilous three days in early July. He had haunted the War Department's telegraph office, studying every dispatch, keeping in constant touch with the Union Army.

On the last day of June in 1863 the prosperous German community of Gettysburg had been a peaceful little village of some twenty-five hundred people. Fertile rolling farmlands and wooded hills surrounded the neat, red brick homes, the seven churches, the college, and the seminary that made up the town.

A dozen roads radiated from Gettysburg, like spokes from the hub of a wagon wheel. General Lee was in southern Pennsylvania with his Confederate forces; General Meade had his men in northern Maryland. In trying to locate each other, the two generals moved their armies along these converging roads. Unexpectedly, they met at Gettysburg. Beginning on the morning of July 1st, the two armies were locked in a terrible struggle that had lasted for three days.

The Confederate Army had withdrawn on the night of July 3rd, leaving the Union Army victorious. But there were more than seven thousand casualties in the surrounding countryside. Some twenty thousand wounded had to be housed in makeshift hospitals: churches, schools, and homes of generous-hearted Gettysburg residents. Even the barns along Rock Creek and Willoughby's Run were converted into temporary quarters for the men who had been shot down in battle. Members of the Sanitary Commission, an organization similar to our modern Red Cross, had moved into the battle area, doing what they could to alleviate the suffering.

Early on the morning of July 4th, burial parties were organized with both citizens and soldiers participating. In a steady downpour of rain, they went out to bury the fallen soldiers who were cluttering the fields. Graves were hastily prepared on the slopes of Culp's Hill, in the Wheatfield, in the woods around Spangler's Spring, and along the battered stone walls of Cemetery Ridge. But six weeks later, the heavy summer rains had washed out hundreds of bodies from their shallow dugouts.

As yet, no national plans had been made for the burial of Civil War soldiers. Until now, most of the Union men had fallen in hostile southern territory. A small number of bodies had been claimed by relatives and sent to their native states for burial.

But the Battle of Gettysburg had posed a different problem. Several thousand Union men had fallen in one area. If a burial ground were to be located here, it would be easily accessible to the well-populated eastern cities.

The Library of Congress

One of the most popular of all photographs showing Mr. Lincoln and his youngest son, Tad. This was one of the rare pictures in which Mr. Lincoln was wearing his spectacles.

By the latter part of August, the little community of Gettysburg seemed to be plagued with an unusual amount of illness. Many people believed that it was because of the shallow burials. Yes, health hazards, too, were beginning to present a serious problem. Something had to be done!

President Lincoln had been told that his good friend, Andrew Curtin, governor of Pennsylvania, had taken the problem under advisement. He had appointed a Gettysburg lawyer, David Wills, to look into the matter. The public-spirited Mr. Wills was pleased to act for the Governor and immediately began making recommendations.

His first suggestion was that a corporation be formed which would be called the National Soldiers' Cemetery. This would be governed by a Board of Commissioners, consisting of one member appointed by each northern governor whose state had lost men at Gettysburg.

Governor Curtin heartily approved the idea of a national burial ground and suggested that Mr. Wills proceed at once to carry out the proposal. The next step was the purchase of land for the cemetery. Mr. Wills selected a seventeen-acre plot on the Baltimore turnpike, at the point where, on July 1st, the Union Army had thrown back the Louisiana Tigers. It was one of the highest spots in the area—a place which commanded a sweeping view of the whole battleground.

Soldiers from eighteen states had been involved in the three-day conflict: soldiers from Maine, New Hampshire, Vermont, Massachusetts, Rhode Island, Connecticut, New York, New Jersey, Pennsylvania, Delaware, Maryland, West Virginia, Ohio, Indiana, Illinois, Michigan, Wisconsin, and Minnesota. The price of the land for the cemetery, maintenance of the grounds, and cost of the burials was to be apportioned to the various states according to the number of representatives they had in Congress. It was not really a fair apportionment, since states like Pennsylvania and New York had lost far more soldiers than Illinois with its six burials. But no one questioned the costs. The governors accepted the plan eagerly, and each appointed a representative for the Board of Commissioners.

At a meeting of the board early in September, it was agreed that the National Cemetery should be dedicated with proper ceremony. October 23, 1863, was chosen as the date. And of course the Honorable Edward Everett must deliver the oration.

Edward Everett was known as the foremost speaker of the day. He was a former secretary of state, United States senator, governor of Massachusetts, and president of Harvard. His career had been a long and illustrious one; his fame as a classical orator had penetrated into every part of the nation. Thousands and thousands of people had heard his oration on "The Character of Washington" delivered many times in many parts of the country. He had donated all proceeds from this lecture to a fund designed for the purchase and preservation of Mount Vernon as a national memorial. Yes, there was no doubt about the fact that Mr. Everett must deliver the oration at the dedication of the National Cemetery.

The sixty-nine-year-old orator was flattered by the invitation to speak at Gettysburg, but replied that the occasion was "not to be dismissed with a few sentimental or patriotic commonplaces." He would need more time for the preparation of such an important speech. Could the date be moved up into November sometime?

The commissioners realized the hazards of bad weather

which might be encountered. Still, the venerable Mr. Everett was an important man and his wishes must be considered. So the dedication date was changed to Thursday, November 19th.

Once the date was decided upon, the board authorized printed invitations to be mailed to hundreds of dignitaries. It was that printed invitation which held Mr. Lincoln's attention on this particular night in mid-October.

The dedication of the National Cemetery at Gettysburg—yes, of course he must go. After he had finished the stack of papers on the table, Mr. Lincoln took out a sheet of Executive Mansion paper and penned a note of acceptance to Mr. Wills.

The President's last chore of the evening was the customary visit to the War Department telegraph office, even though the hour was late. He often thought how fortunate it was that the War Department Building was so close, just across the street on Executive Avenue. Slipping down the narrow private stairway at the west end of the second floor, the President hustled across the wooded lawn, noting with some pleasure that the leaves were almost gone from the trees. Now, at least, those Confederate "bushwhackers" couldn't hide in the foliage of the nearby countryside and pick off unsuspecting Union soldiers.

In the telegraph office the operators stacked the military telegrams in a specific desk drawer with the latest message placed on top. Mr. Lincoln always took out the stack and looked over each message carefully until he came to the ones he had seen before. His position while reading the telegrams never varied; he sat far forward on his chair with one knee practically touching the floor. He finished reading the telegrams and returned them to the desk drawer.

As he walked slowly back to the White House, Mr. Lincoln was glad he had accepted the invitation to go to Gettysburg. This would be his opportunity to pay silent tribute to the brave men who had died there.

Perhaps there was another reason for the President's acceptance of the invitation. On October 1, 1862, he had visited Antietam with General McClellan, surveying the field where a great battle had been fought on September 17. A member of the press reported that Mr. Lincoln had laughed and joked at the scene and had asked his companion, Ward Hill Lamon, to sing a comic song.

It was a completely false and malicious report, but it received wide circulation throughout the country, particularly in the anti-Lincoln newspapers. General McClellan could easily have denied the story; however, he did not choose to do so. And when the news reporter was questioned later about the incident, he said that nobody really believed it. But it was "the kind of stuff" you had to write. The President was hurt, deeply hurt, although he never made any public statement about the lie.

When the commissioners received Mr. Lincoln's acceptance, they were frankly surprised. Few people had even bothered to reply and the President's letter was completely unexpected. Colonel Clark E. Carr, the Illinois member of the board, suggested that perhaps Mr. Lincoln should be invited to speak at the dedication.

Most of the board members had never heard the President speak. They knew he had great ability as a political orator.

The reports of his debates with Senator Douglas and his Cooper Union Address were proof of that fact. But several of the members raised questions about whether he could make appropriate remarks on such a solemn occasion as the memorial service. Besides, they argued, with his many other important duties, would Mr. Lincoln have time to prepare an address for the dedication?

Colonel Carr insisted that the President should be the person to make this decision, and that, if he accepted, he would be sure to say the right thing under the circumstances. It was finally decided that the board would ask Mr. Lincoln to say a few words when Mr. Everett had finished. David Wills was instructed to issue the invitation to the President.

Scarcely two weeks before the dedication, Mr. Lincoln received a second invitation—this time, a letter written by Mr. Wills and dated November 2, 1863. It read:

> The several states having soldiers in the Army of the Potomac, who were killed at the battle of Gettysburg, or have since died at the various hospitals which were established in the vicinity, have procured grounds on a prominent part of the battlefield for a cemetery, and are having the dead removed to them, and properly buried. These grounds will be consecrated and set apart to this sacred purpose, by appropriate ceremonies, on Thursday, the 19th instant. Hon. Edward Everett will deliver the oration. I am authorized by the Governors of the different states to invite you to be present and participate in these ceremonies, which will doubtless be very imposing and solemnly impressive. It is the desire that after the oration,

> you, as Chief Executive of the Nation, formally set apart these grounds to their sacred use by a few appropriate remarks. It will be a source of great gratification to the many widows and orphans that have been made almost friendless by the great battle here, to have you here personally. . . . We hope you will be able to be present to perform this last solemn act to the soldier-dead on this battlefield.

Mr. Wills also included a private note to the President, asking that Mr. Lincoln be his personal guest during the Gettysburg visit. Governor Curtin and the Honorable Edward Everett would also be staying with him, he added.

Mr. Lincoln was fully aware that Edward Everett had been a vice-presidential candidate on the Constitutional Union Party ticket, one of the opposition parties in 1860. However, after the election, Mr. Everett had publicly declared that he now fully supported the present administration. The two men had met only a few times. They didn't really know each other, although in September, 1863, the President had written a note of introduction for Mr. Everett's forthcoming trip to Europe, saying that Everett "bears no mission from this government, and yet no gentleman is better able to correct misunderstandings in the minds of foreigners in regard to American affairs." Contemplating the note from Mr. Wills, Mr. Lincoln decided that some time spent with the venerable statesman might prove to be an interesting experience.

The fact that Governor Curtin would be at Mr. Wills' home pleased the President even more. Andrew Curtin's enthusiastic support at the Republican Convention in 1860 had been greatly appreciated. Without it, Mr. Lincoln knew he probably would never have been nominated. Yes, it would be good to see Governor Curtin again.

For the second time, Mr. Lincoln wrote an acceptance to Mr. Wills, agreeing to make the "few appropriate remarks" which the invitation had specified. It would be a privilege, he thought, to pay tribute to the brave men, both the living and the dead, who had fought so valiantly at Gettysburg. If he could just find the right words—someway. Somehow he *must* find the right words to assuage the grief of the mourning kinfolk.

Although the second invitation was definitely an afterthought on the part of the board, it never occurred to President Lincoln to be offended.

TWO

So Many Interruptions

TIME was closing in on Mr. Lincoln. He felt a sense of urgency about those "few appropriate remarks" for the dedication at Gettysburg. Saying just the right thing was very important; yet how could one devote much time to speech writing when there were many more pressing matters?

Strategy for the war was an ever-present problem. And the President was spending long hours at the War Department, keeping in touch with General Grant at Chattanooga. Since this would be the setting fot the next big engagement, a flurry of telegrams arrived daily.

The Annual Message for Congress must be prepared too. The President was glad that he would be able to tell Congress that "actual commencement of work upon the Pacific railroad" had begun. And there was that endless flow of callers who climbed the White House stairs every day. A veteran White House employe, Louis Bargdorf, stood guard in the upstairs hall but he seemed to have little influence on those who came and went. The secretaries, John Nicolay and John Hay, tried to weed out the unimportant callers. Somehow, though, most of the visitors managed to get into Mr. Lincoln's office. They were a curious cross section, these people who wanted to talk with the President, the humble as well as the famous.

Mr. Lincoln's usual greeting was a pleasant, "How do you do?" or "Well, friend, what can I do for you?" Strangers were instantly put at ease by the innate courtesy and kindly manner. As the interview proceeded, the President would lean forward slightly in his chair, his long legs crossed easily, listening intently to his caller. He could not always grant the requests, but he sometimes softened the refusal with a quip. When a man asked him for a pass to Richmond, instead of bluntly saying no, the President remarked, "I would gladly give you the pass if it would do any good, but in the last two years I have given passes to Richmond to 250,000 men and not one of them has managed to get there yet."

There were times, however, when Mr. Lincoln could, and did, take action on the problem presented to him. This action often took the form of a terse presidential note, occasionally reflecting his wry sense of humor, such as the one he wrote to Major George Ramsey, Commandant of the Washington Arsenal. The note read: "The lady—bearer of this—says she has two sons who want to work. Set them at it, if possible. Wanting to work is so rare a merit, that it should be encouraged."

National Park Service

Pennsylvania Avenue as it appeared in the early 1860's with the unfinished Capitol dome looming up in the distance.

There were so many pleas, so many demands on President Lincoln's time. Yet he seldom lost patience. "If I do get up a little temper," he once observed, "I have no time to keep it up."

Although he had not yet written anything on paper for his Gettysburg speech, Mr. Lincoln was probably putting phrases together in his mind whenever there was a quiet moment. Those were the days before the president of the United States was surrounded with speech writers and research men. The words of the Gettysburg Address would be Mr. Lincoln's alone.

Less than one year of formal schooling was not much preparation for a presidential speech. But Abraham Lincoln was a man who had never ceased studying. The plays of William Shakespeare, the poems of Robert Burns, the fables of Aesop, and the Bible—most particularly the Bible, were the books the President had read and reread. He was to find his thoughts turning more and more to a Biblical rhythm as he tried to plan his "few appropriate remarks."

The occasion would be a solemn one; Mr. Wills had made that very clear. And the few remarks would dedicate the ground to "its sacred purpose." But on one point Mr. Lincoln was very certain. He could not be vindictive about the South. The President had never found it in his sympathetic heart to be bitter towards the Confederate soldiers. No, there must be a timelessness about these remarks. He must find some way to emphasize the importance of a great democracy, perhaps even to challenge the generations to come. Yes, this speech would be work—but it would be well worth the effort.

Secretary John Nicolay reported in his diary that the President was pursuing his "usual custom of using great deliberation in arranging his thoughts and moulding his phrases, mentally, waiting to reduce them to writing 'til they had taken satisfactory form."

There were social affairs that had to be attended too. On Thursday evening, November 12th, Kate Chase, the daughter of Mr. Lincoln's Secretary of the Treasury, was being married to the Rhode Island governor, William Sprague. It was a brilliant ceremony to which all the socially and politically elite of Washington had been invited. People were saying that Kate's marriage was one of political importance, a marriage which should advance her father's political ambitions. Mrs. Lincoln had refused to go, so the President went alone, taking a dainty little fan as a gift for the bride. Undoubtedly, he felt it was better to be present at the affair than to stir up a controversy because he hadn't come.

Interruption followed interruption. The next day there was a special presentation. Senator John Conness of California called at the White House with a gold-mounted cane for Mr. Lincoln. And the President responded with a brief speech. Then on Saturday, the 14th, a South American pony was delivered to Tad—a gift from Colonel Joseph B. Stewart. Of course, "Papa-Day" had to join the boy's inspection in the White House stable.

The November days were slipping away rapidly. Mr. Lincoln was glad, though, that he had already completed the Thanksgiving proclamation. Mrs. Sarah Hale, the editor of *Godey's Lady's Book*, had been very persistent in her efforts to have the President establish an annual Thanksgiving Day.

He had listened to her pleas with a sympathetic ear. Yes, it was good to know that the country would now have an established day each year in which to give thanks to God for such bountiful blessings.

A few days before departing for the dedication, Mr. Lincoln contacted his long-time Negro friend, William Johnson, who was now working as a janitor in the Treasury Department. William had served as valet on the long two-week train trip from Springfield to Washington in 1861. His care of the President's wardrobe and his devotion to Mr. Lincoln won commendation from Henry Villard, a news reporter on the trip. Mr. Villard in the *New York Herald* of February 29, 1861, wrote that William "although not exactly the most prominent, is yet the most useful member of the party."

Mr. Lincoln had hoped to use William as his valet at the White House, but the Negroes who were already installed made violent objections. It seemed there was a long-standing tradition that only light-skinned Negroes could serve in the White House. So the President had bowed to the wishes of the household staff and had found William a job in the Treasury Department.

Occasionally the President asked the Department to give William a short leave of absence so he might accompany Mr. Lincoln on out-of-town trips in his former capacity as valet. This was just such an occasion. William was pleased to be invited and accepted Mr. Lincoln's invitation with undisguised pleasure.

On Sunday, November 15, the President had an appointment with Alexander Gardner, photographer, whose gallery was located on Seventh Street. Mr. Lincoln asked Noah

The Library of Congress

The gallery of the photographer who took Mr. Lincoln's picture on Sunday, November 15, 1863.

Brooks, a newspaper correspondent and long-time friend, to accompany him. He was careful to explain that Sunday was the only time he could go, since any other day would interfere with "the public business." Besides, by choosing Sunday, the President hoped that he would not be besieged by curiosity seekers "and other seekers," while they walked along the street.

As the two men passed through the front entrance of the White House, Mr. Lincoln nodded pleasantly to Edward Moran, the short, thin Irishman who had stood guard at the door since the days of President Taylor.

Striding along Pennsylvania Avenue, Mr. Brooks brought up the subject of the coming dedication at Gettysburg, asking if Mr. Lincoln had written his speech yet. The President explained that it was written "but not finished." He also added that he was keeping his remarks short, short, short.

Once they arrived at Gardner's Gallery, the President was kept busy posing for the various sittings which photographer Gardner had planned. There was no time to think about the speech he had to prepare.

Even on this particular November Sunday, the aggressive office seekers were not to be put off. Returning to the White House, the President and Mr. Brooks walked up the driveway toward the north portico. A gentleman was waiting with a paper covered by endorsements. Mr. Lincoln managed a wry smile. "Office hunting is in the air," he said.

The newspapers had gotten wind of the President's intention to go to the Gettysburg dedication. Editors who were not in sympathy with Mr. Lincoln were proclaiming that the President intended to make "political hay" by speaking over the graves of the dead soldiers. Enemies in Washington were saying that Mr. Lincoln only wanted to put himself in a more favorable light with Governor Curtin and the Pennsylvania politicians.

Mr. Lincoln was well aware of these criticisms. The press was often vitriolic about him. Yet this was an opportunity to prove his faith in the Union. As President, he felt he must take great care in any public statements. He continued doggedly trying to find just the right words. Whenever there was a spare moment, his thoughts turned to those "few appropriate remarks."

Meanwhile, preparations were going forward in the little community of Gettysburg. Ward Hill Lamon, United States Marshal for the District of Columbia, had been appointed chief marshal for the dedication ceremony. It was a job well suited to the talents of the barrel-chested, burly official. People sometimes wondered at the attachment between the blustering Lamon and the gentle, soft-spoken President. Ward Hill Lamon had been Mr. Lincoln's law partner during his Danville, Illinois, days. They had ridden the circuit together, developing a deep and lasting friendship.

When the President-elect left Springfield, he had asked Lamon to accompany him to Washington. Lamon had never forgotten what Jesse K. Dubois, State Auditor of Illinois, had said just as they were leaving: "Lamon, we entrust the sacred life of Mr. Lincoln to your keeping. If you don't protect it, never return to Illinois, for we will murder you on sight." Although spoken in a jocular tone, the statement nevertheless revealed the high regard in which Mr. Lincoln was held by his Illinois friends.

After the Civil War began, Lamon acted as a personal bodyguard to the President. The marshal was sure there were cranks and misguided southern patriots who would welcome the opportunity to kill Mr. Lincoln. Because of these apprehensions, Lamon often slept outside the President's bedroom, rolled up in a blanket on the floor and equipped with pistols, knives, and brass knuckles. "This boy wants me to sit in his lap all day," the President once told a friend. Nevertheless, he was deeply appreciative of the devotion of his junior law partner.

There were times, however, when Mr. Lincoln chided his former partner for his belligerent actions as United States Marshal. In trying to break up what he thought was an illegal street-corner rally, Lamon had almost killed one of the agitators. The President told him, "Hereafter, when you have occasion to strike a man, don't hit him with your fist; strike him with a club or a crowbar or something that won't kill him."

Now, to refute the reported incident at the Antietam Battlefield, Mr. Lincoln had asked that Lamon be chief marshal for the parade to the cemetery—that he introduce the President at the dedication ceremony. Mr. Lincoln wanted to make a second public appearance with Ward Hill Lamon, one that even the anti-Lincoln press could not criticize.

On November 13 Lamon went to Gettysburg and established his headquarters at the Eagle Hotel. He needed some extra time in which to work out the parade route. Then, too, there were numerous assistant marshals who must be instructed on how to form up a parade.

Accompanying Lamon was Benjamin B. French, the Offi-

The Library of Congress

Mr. Lincoln as he was photographed by Alexander Gardner on Sunday, November 14, four days before making his "few appropriate remarks" at Gettysburg.

cer in Charge of Buildings in Washington. When the two men arrived in Gettysburg, they had a long chat with David Wills to cover the details of the dedication. During the course of the conversation Mr. Wills happened to mention that the Board of Commissioners had wanted to have a poem written and set to music especially for this occasion. Lowell, Longfellow, Whittier, Bryant, and George Boker had all been asked to write the poem, but none of these gentlemen had agreed to do so. Mr. Wills reported that the board was very much disappointed at the poets' obvious indifference.

Benjamin B. French fancied himself an amateur poet of sorts, and the next morning before leaving Gettysburg, he handed a manuscript to Mr. Wills. There hadn't been much time, he explained, but he had managed to write a little hymn. He hoped it would be all right.

On Tuesday morning, November 17, the cabinet held its regular meeting in the President's second-floor office. While the gentlemen were seated around the large oak table in the center of the room, President Lincoln brought up the subject of the proposed trip to Gettysburg.

Secretary of War Stanton declined to go because of the gravity of war maneuvers around Chattanooga. Secretary of Navy Welles begged off with the excuse that official business would keep him in Washington. Both men insisted that they could not leave the city, even for one day. However, Secretary of State William H. Seward, Secretary of the Interior John P. Usher, and Postmaster-General Montgomery Blair agreed to make the trip. Secretary of Treasury Salmon P. Chase was absent from the meeting. Mr. Lincoln wrote him a personal note: "I expected to see you here at Cabinet meeting, and to say something about going to Gettysburg. There will be a train to take and return us. The time for starting is not yet fixed; but when it shall be, I will notify you." Secretary Chase had other things on his mind and declined to go.

It was during this Tuesday morning Cabinet meeting that President Lincoln asked Secretary Stanton to arrange for a special train. Later that day the Secretary sent a note to the White House, suggesting that the Baltimore and Ohio Railroad would have a special train leaving Washington at 6 A.M. on Thursday morning. Connections along the line would be so arranged that the train would wait in Gettysburg and return Mr. Lincoln and his party to Washington, leaving at 6 P.M., "thus," as the Secretary noted, "doing all in one day." He concluded the note by adding:

"Please consider it, and if any change is desired, let me know, so that it can be made."

Mr. Lincoln was not at all pleased. He returned Secretary Stanton's letter with the notation: "I do not like this arrangement. I do not wish to so go that by the slightest accident we fail entirely, and, at the best, the whole to be a mere breathless running of the gauntlet."

Mr. Stanton immediately changed the plans. The special train would leave the Baltimore and Ohio Station at noon on Wednesday, November 18. Railway officials were notified of the new time and the President was apparently well pleased with the revised arrangement.

A number of people thought that Thaddeus Stevens, the Republican floor leader in the House of Representatives would certainly be going to the dedication ceremony. He was a Pennsylvania politician and had at one time during his career practiced law in Gettysburg. When someone asked Mr. Stevens if he were going, he gave an emphatic no and added that he thought that Abraham Lincoln was indeed a "dead card in the current political deck."

An hour or so of Mr. Lincoln's time on that Tuesday afternoon was consumed by having to review a parade of twenty-five hundred men from the Invalid Corps. The President believed this was time well-spent, though, since he was deeply in sympathy with the Invalid Corps. Its members were recruited from the army hospitals. If a wounded soldier was permanently unfit for further field service but could still be somewhat active, he could, if he wished, enlist in the Invalid Corps. These men were given duty as guards at prison camps, hospitals, and military arsenals. The more active soldiers in the field sometimes made fun of the men in the Invalid Corps, and the name in particular became quite a source of irritation. Eventually it was changed to "Veteran Reserve Corps."

On that same Tuesday afternoon Mr. Lincoln also received the Honorable James Speed for an interview. A number of years later Attorney Speed recalled that he had asked about the President's speech, whether it was written as yet. And Mr. Lincoln had replied that he had found time to write "only about half of it."

After dinner on Tuesday evening, November 17, William Saunders, Superintendent of Grounds in the Agriculture Department, went to the White House at President Lincoln's request. He had drawn up plans for the new Gettysburg Cemetery and Mr. Lincoln was anxious to see them.

Mr. Saunders reported that when he spread the plans out on the President's table, Mr. Lincoln showed great interest in the drawings. He seemed very familiar with Culp's Hill, Little Round Top, and the surrounding territory, although he had never visited Gettysburg.

Mr. Lincoln liked the plan. The cemetery was designed in a half-circle with the graves laid out by states and a uniform headstone for each. In the center, Mr. Saunders had indicated a space to be reserved for a monument which would be erected at a later date. When the interview was over, the President told Mr. Saunders that he hoped to see him on the train the following afternoon.

Exactly when Mr. Lincoln had time to write out his address is not known. However, we do know that at least part of it was written before he left for Gettysburg. Page one of the first draft was inscribed on Executive Mansion stationery.

And now the time of departure was only a few hours away!

THREE

On the Train to Gettysburg

WEDNESDAY, November 18, began much as any other day did at the White House. Being a fitful sleeper, Mr. Lincoln was usually up before six o'clock. Today was no exception. When breakfast was announced, he had already put in a good hour of work.

However, by seven-thirty the household was in an uproar. Tad was sick. After making his examination, the doctor only shook his head, much as he had done when Willie was ill. The grave indecision about Tad's condition threw Mrs. Lincoln into a state of hysterics. The President simply couldn't go running off to Gettysburg. He knew very well that Tad wouldn't take his medicine for anyone but Pa! And did he think more of that old battlefield than he did his own flesh and blood?

This was one of the few times that Mr. Lincoln felt he must go against his wife's wishes. He had promised to be present at the dedication ceremony and nothing could change his mind. He kept telling himself that he must have faith that Tad would be all right. Besides, he could keep in touch by telegraph wire.

The War Department had detailed General James B. Fry to escort the President to Gettysburg. When General Fry arrived at the north portico of the White House shortly before noon, he found the President still wasn't quite ready. Somewhat impatiently the General tried to hurry Mr. Lincoln into the waiting carriage. There was no time to be lost, the General insisted.

In his calm unruffled manner, the President recalled that he felt like the man he had heard about back in Illinois. This man, he said, was on his way to be hanged. But the people kept pushing and shoving, blocking the passageway so that it was almost impossible to get through the crowd. Finally the doomed fellow called out, "Boys, you needn't be in such a hurry. There won't be any fun till I get there."

The War Department carriage jounced along over the rough cobblestones of Pennsylvania Avenue, cobblestones that were rutted and broken from the endless lines of army wagons and artillery pieces that had moved into the city. Mr. Lincoln peered out of the carriage window, looking toward the nearly completed Capitol dome which loomed up against the sky. He remembered how the Confederates had claimed that the dome would never be finished until they had won the war and could finish it themselves.

The President was glad he had insisted that work on the dome continue despite the war. There had been a great deal of criticism about using men and materials to work on the Capitol dome. But Mr. Lincoln had stood firm. This construction, he had said, was "a sign we intend the Union shall go on."

There was a great deal of satisfaction in knowing that the gigantic three-tiered dome would soon be finished. Thomas Crawford's mighty bronze goddess would then be hoisted up to the top of the dome's lantern structure. In less than three weeks, the last of the statue's five sections would be bolted into place.

Quite a crowd was on hand by the time the carriage reached the Baltimore and Ohio's ornate wooden station at the corner of New Jersey Avenue and C Street. Since the tracks were on the street level, it was not hard to find the Presidential Special.

Huffing and panting through its huge funnel-shaped stack, the locomotive William Mason, No. 25 seemed to be waiting rather impatiently at the head of the four-car special train. The tender was piled full of cordwood; steam was hissing out in voluminous clouds.

The Baltimore and Ohio officials had ordered the sides of the engine decorated with red, white, and blue bunting. Flags had been attached to the glass-enclosed kerosene light on the front, giving a gala appearance to what was otherwise supposed to be a somber mission. Four wooden passenger cars made up the train. The rear third of the last car had been temporarily converted into a drawing room for the President and his close associates.

In addition to a number of news correspondents and a Military Guard of Honor, there were several diplomatic dignitaries who were also boarding the train. The French Minister, M. Mercier, and Admiral Renaud of the French Navy were there, along with Chevalier Bertinatti, the Italian Minister, and Mr. McDougall, who represented the Canadian Ministry.

The First Regiment of the Invalid Corps had sent an escort. Colonel George W. Burton and Captain Alan Ramsey represented the Marine Corps. The Marine Band also trooped aboard, with Lieutenant Henry Clay Cochrane in charge. And Mr. Lincoln had made a special point of inviting Navy Captain and Mrs. H.A. Wise to ride the Special, since Mrs. Wise was the daughter of the dedication orator, Edward Everett.

Shortly after twelve the train pulled away from the station, picking up speed as it snorted and chugged down the tracks. In the drawing room with the President were his three cabinet members, Seward, Usher and Blair; William Johnson, the colored valet; and the private secretaries, John Nicolay and John Hay. Soon after the trip began, Lieutenant Cochrane came into the drawing room with a copy of the *New York Herald* and suggested that the President might like to take a look at it.

Thanking the Lieutenant, Mr. Lincoln added, "I like to see what they say about us." The paper had accounts of Burnside at Knoxville, Sherman at Chattanooga, and Meade's activities on the Rapidan. After some little time, the President began to laugh and remarked about what wild guesses the newsmen could make concerning the next war moves. Lieutenant Cochrane was pleased to see the President's face light up. He seemed so sad and careworn.

The Library of Congress

The unfinished Capitol dome as it probably looked to Mr. Lincoln when he passed it on the way to the Baltimore and Ohio station on November 18, 1863.

As the train rocked along, Mr. Lincoln observed that there was quite a difference now in the vessels on the Chesapeake. When he had first come to Congress in 1847, he had noted that there were square-rigged vessels "up the Patapsco River as far as the Relay House." But times had changed, he added. Now there seemed to be only small vessels.

When the Presidential Special neared the outskirts of Baltimore, Secretary Seward became obviously uneasy. Mr. Lincoln had not been through Baltimore since his inaugural in 1861. The city was known to be a hot-bed of secessionists, a meeting place for radicals who were anxious to do away with President Lincoln.

Secretary Seward was all too familiar with the details of the suspected Baltimore Plot, when the secessionists had planned to kill Mr. Lincoln as he passed through the city on his way to the inauguration. The plot had been discovered by Detective Allan Pinkerton, and arrangements were made to whisk the President-elect through the city in the early morning hours, well ahead of his scheduled arrival time.

Mr. Lincoln had been incredulous at the idea that anyone should want to kill him. However, the evidence had seemed so overwhelming that he had submitted to the secret plans and had arrived in Washington without incident. Nevertheless, Secretary Seward knew that there was still strong secessionist feeling in Baltimore. He was definitely worried about the trip through the city.

At one-twenty P.M. the Presidential Special steamed into Baltimore's Camden Station, just one hour and ten minutes after leaving Washington. Mr. J.W. Garrett, president of the Baltimore and Ohio, and Mr. J.D. Cameron, president of

GEORGETOWN

National Park Service

The Baltimore and Ohio Railroad Station at New Jersey and C Street, Northwest, from which Mr. Lincoln's special train departed on Wednesday, November 18, 1863.

the Northern Central Railroad, were on hand to greet Mr. Lincoln.

These were the days before a single station served all the railroads in one city. It was customary for passenger cars to be detached from the locomotive in one station and hauled by dray horses across town to another station. While the horses were being hitched up to the passenger cars, the Marine Band piled out of the train and entertained the spectators with some lively music.

Progress up the long Howard Street hill was slow as the horses tugged and pulled the heavy passenger cars along the street. The sidewalks were thronged with people who cheered enthusiastically as the cars passed. Several times along the way Mr. Lincoln went to the rear platform and waved to the crowds. Secretary of State Seward was relieved that everyone seemed so friendly. The secessionist radicals were not in evidence.

At the Northern Central's Bolton Station, another locomotive was attached. A crowd of about two hundred people had assembled on the station platform. They began calling for the President to appear. When Mr. Lincoln stepped outside, two mothers with babies in their arms thrust the tots toward the President. He took each one in turn and kissed him gently.

Major General Robert C. Schenck and his staff boarded the train at the Bolton Station and a fifth car was attached to the Special. It was a baggage car which had been converted into a diner so that the passengers might have some lunch. President Lincoln joined the luncheon group and sat at the head of the table.

The train steamed out of Baltimore on the Northern Central tracks, jolting and lurching its way toward Hanover Junction, Pennsylvania. After lunch Mr. Lincoln walked into one of the passenger cars and sat down with a group of men who were telling stories. Obviously enjoying himself, the President took his turn and related a number of yarns from his early years. After about an hour he excused himself, saying that he must go back to his car. "The people," he explained, "will expect me to say something to them tomorrow, and I must give the matter some thought."

The wail of the engine's steam whistle and the clang of the big brass bell heralded the stop at Hanover Junction. As the train ground to a halt, someone lifted a little girl clutching a bouquet of rosebuds up to the open window of Mr. Lincoln's private car. "Flowerth for the Prethident," she lisped.

Graciously Mr. Lincoln accepted the flowers. Then he stooped over and kissed the little girl on the cheek, saying, "You're a sweet little rosebud yourself."

While the train was taking on wood and water at Hanover Junction, an old man climbed aboard and went into the drawing room to shake the President's hand. He told Mr. Lincoln that he had had a boy who was killed at Little Round Top during the Battle of Gettysburg.

The sad-eyed President gave the old man a compassionate look. "When I think," he said, "of the sacrifices of life yet to be offered, and the hearts and homes yet to be made desolate before this dreadful war is over, my heart is like lead within me, and I feel at times like hiding in deep darkness."

At Hanover Junction the train was switched over to the Western Maryland tracks. It was just beginning to pick up speed when, once again, the wheels ground to a screeching halt—this time to let an east-bound train pass by, a military train which was always given the right-of-way during war time.

During this unexpected stop, a small crowd quickly gathered around the train, calling insistently for the President. Mr. Lincoln stepped out on the back platform. "Well," he said, smiling, "you've seen me and according to general experience you've seen less than you expected to see." He was given a resounding cheer.

Once the train started up again, it seemed to rock and sway at a perilous angle as it covered the last thirty miles to Gettysburg. During the final hour of the trip, Wayne MacVeagh, chairman of the Pennsylvania Republican Central Committee, came into the President's private car and chatted with Mr. Lincoln about his policy in Missouri. A factional fight had developed among the Missouri Republicans and Mr. Lincoln was doing his best to mediate matters. MacVeagh's remarks were not particularly complimentary about the administration's actions.

With all the conversation, the stops, the impromptu speeches, and the interruptions, there had been no time to work on those "few appropriate remarks" for tomorrow. Anyway, the jolting and lurching of the train made writing a virtually impossible feat. If Mr. Lincoln had done any thinking about his speech, he had not put the thoughts on paper.

And now William Johnson, the colored valet, was flicking dust off the President's black stovepipe hat. The train was slowing down for its final stop. The Gettysburg station on Carlisle Street was just around the bend.

FOUR

Wednesday Evening in Gettysburg

A LARGE crowd of people had gathered at the Carlisle Street Station after word leaked out that the Presidential Special would arrive around five. For several hours Mr. Lincoln's admirers, as well as the curious, had been milling about the platform. Movement was somewhat restricted, though, by the piles of wooden coffins that were stacked neatly alongside the tracks. Some parents had decided that Gettysburg was too far away—had asked that their boys be sent home. Officials were doing their best to keep up with the requests. Despite the celebration mood of the crowd, the rough pine boxes were a sobering reminder of those three terrible days last July.

Commissioner David Wills and General Darius Couch

were on hand as a welcoming committee for the incoming dignitaries. Edward Everett had insisted upon coming to the station too. His primary concern was for his daughter, Mrs. Wise, although he did profess an interest in meeting Mr. Lincoln. Shortly before five, a Guard of Honor from the Invalid Corps arrived at the station to form an escort for its Commander-in-chief.

When the Presidential Special braked to a stop, people began streaming out of the wooden passenger cars. Mr. Everett was relieved to see that his daughter had arrived safely.

Mr. Wills stepped forward to greet the President as he alighted from the rear car. The Commissioner pointed out that his carriage was waiting for Mr. Lincoln, but the President insisted on first walking forward to the front of the train to shake hands with the engineer, a gesture which pleased the watching crowd.

Accompanied by the Honor Guard, the Wills carriage bearing the presidential party moved slowly away from the railroad station. As they rode through the street Mr. Lincoln noted that many people were lined up along the sidewalks. Some merely gawked, but for the most part, the spectators were cheering and waving while the dignitaries passed.

Although the town of Gettysburg boasted a hotel, of sorts, Mr. Wills had decided that his own home would offer better accommodations to the important visitors. Located on "The Diamond," a name which Gettysburg citizens had given to their public square, the Wills' house was a large three-story brick rectangle, reputedly one of the finest homes in Gettysburg.

Edward Everett was already installed in one of the bedrooms on the Wills' second floor. He had arrived three days ago for the express purpose of checking out the battlefield. Before he began writing his oration, Mr. Everett had requested detailed accounts of the battle from General Meade. Nothing could be left to chance. He had come to Gettysburg on Monday in order to familiarize himself with the vast area which had been covered in the three-day battle. Every topographical allusion in his speech must be geographically correct. And the elderly gentleman had spent many hours walking through the area. In fact, he had just returned from Seminary Ridge in time to join his host at the railroad station.

Now the party was alighting from the carriage on the York Street side of the Wills house. The Commissioner was introducing his next-door neighbor, Mr. R.G. Harper, editor of Gettysburg's weekly, the *Adams County Sentinel.* In making arrangements for all the distinguished guests, Mr. Wills had run out of bedrooms in his own house. He was sorry, he explained, but Secretary of State Seward would have to stay with Mr. Harper, whose home adjoined the Wills house on the public square.

A few minutes later, Mr. Lincoln and his valet, William, were shown to a bedroom on the second floor. The flickering light from the gas chandelier revealed a room that was tastefully appointed, although a spacious four-poster canopy bed seemed to dwarf the other furnishings in the room: the marble-topped mahogany chest, the wash-stand in the corner, the high-backed velvet chair, and the little spool-legged table which Mr. Lincoln would appropriate later in the evening as a desk.

Moving quietly but efficiently, William unpacked the President's bag and smoothed out the creases in the suit

The Lane Studio, Gettysburg, Pa.

The David Wills home in Gettysburg. Mr. Lincoln was a guest here on the night of November 18, 1863. To the right is the home of Mr. R. G. Harper, where Secretary of State Seward was entertained.

which Mr. Lincoln would wear for Mrs. Wills' dinner party. This quiet efficiency was one of the reasons Mr. Lincoln enjoyed having William around. The valet didn't keep up a running stream of conversation; yet he anticipated his employer's slightest need.

As he finished dressing for dinner, Mr. Lincoln heard some commotion outside—shouts and cheers, mingled with singing and laughter. He went to the bedroom window which faced on the public square. Pulling aside the heavy lace curtains, the President could see crowds of people milling aimlessly around in The Diamond.

Mr. Wills had told him that strangers had been arriving in Gettysburg ever since Monday: people from New York and Baltimore, from Philadelphia, Pittsburgh, and Washington. Trains had been steaming into the Carlisle Street Station every few hours. In fact, there was such an influx of passenger travel that the railroads had exhausted their supply of passenger cars. They had resorted to freight boxcars, setting up rough boards as seats in order to accommodate the thousands who wanted passage to Gettysburg.

The dedication ceremony was the principal attraction, of course. Some were coming out of curiosity; some wanted to explore the battlefield; others were attracted by the many men of national prominence who would attend the ceremony. And there were those who wanted to be present simply to pay tribute to the soldiers who had fallen in that great battle. Whatever their reasons, almost fifteen thousand people had invaded the little community. Now, it looked as if every stranger in town had decided to join the crowd in the public square.

Turning away from the window, Mr. Lincoln left his room

and walked slowly down the stairway to join the distinguished group in the front parlor. Mrs. David Wills was a gracious hostess, providing both a delicious meal and stimulating conversation. The guest of honor that evening proved he was anything but "the boorish backwoods President" that his critics liked to claim. Speaking at Revere House in Boston several months afterward, Edward Everett assured his audience that at the Wills' dinner party he had watched Mr. Lincoln closely—that in appearance, conversation, and manners he was "the peer of any person present."

Before the guests had left the dinner table, the hubbub in the public square became unbearably noisy. A serenading party had been formed, headed by the New York Fifth Artillery Band. The hastily organized group stopped in front of Mr. Wills' home and began calling for the President.

Mr. Lincoln hesitated about going outside. He didn't like to make impromptu speeches. Anything he said in public was usually written out and carefully worked over beforehand. He knew he was not a good off-the-cuff speaker. But the cries became more and more insistent.

Finally the President stepped out on the small porch which faced York Street. When the crowd quieted down, he said, "I appear before you, fellow citizens, merely to thank you for this compliment. The inference is a very fair one that you would hear me for a little while at least, were I to commence to make a speech. I do not appear before you for the purpose of doing so, and for several substantial reasons. The most substantial of these is that I have no speech to make. In my position it is sometimes important that I should not say any foolish things . . ." An impertinent voice in the crowd interrupted, "If you can help it."

And Mr. Lincoln finished up quickly, "It very often happens that the only way to help it is to say nothing at all. Believing that is my present condition this evening, I must beg of you to excuse me from addressing you further."

As he turned to go back into the house, Mr. Lincoln knew he hadn't said the right thing, that most people didn't understand his particular brand of humor. He was glad Mrs. Lincoln hadn't been there. She would probably have told him, as she often did, that she was so mortified by what he had said, she just wished the ground would swallow her up.

The serenading party moved on to the house next door, calling loudly for the Secretary of State. Mr. Seward obliged with a longer speech than Mr. Lincoln's. The more he talked, the more he warmed to his subject, dwelling on the hope that the North and the South would soon be reconciled. He closed by saying, "Then we shall know that we are not enemies, that we are friends and brothers, that this Union is a reality, and we shall mourn together for the evil wrought by this rebellion."

It was such a beautiful night, warm and clear, real Indian summer weather with a bright full moon that shone down on the roving populace. The serenaders were in no mood to disperse, so they rambled on through the town, seeking out other notables who would say a few words. They had no problems with the politicians; Representatives McPherson and McKnight, Judge Shannon and Wayne MacVeagh gladly obliged their callers with speeches.

When Mr. Lincoln rejoined the Wills dinner guests, he was informed that a telegram had been delivered for him from Secretary of War Stanton. A broad smile spread across the tired face as he read, "On inquiry, Mrs. Lincoln informs me that your son is better this evening." Now, at least one major worry had been eased.

Soon after nine o'clock, Mr. Lincoln excused himself, telling the guests that he must go to his room and do some more work on his remarks for the dedication. When he started up the stairway, the President was followed by a young sergeant, H.P. Bigham, a member of Company B, Twenty-first Pennsylvania Volunteer Cavalry. Sergeant Bigham had been detailed to stand guard at the President's bedroom door throughout the night. He was now reporting for duty.

The valet, William Johnson, sprang up from his chair when Mr. Lincoln opened the door. After helping the President remove his coat, William pulled up the only straight-backed chair in the room and placed it beside the fragile-looking spool-legged table. Mr. Lincoln's legs were too long to fit underneath the table; he was forced to lean over awkwardly as he began jotting down words and sentences for his "few appropriate remarks."

At about ten o'clock the President asked William to go downstairs and find Mr. Wills. There were a few questions he wanted to ask his host.

Mr. Wills came up immediately and the President questioned him about the arrangements for tomorrow's dedication, asking explicitly about the part he was to take. The Commissioner detailed the proposed march to the battlefield and the order of the ceremony itself. A number of years later Mr. Wills told friends that the President did not ask him for writing paper, that he noticed, in particular, that Mr. Lincoln had brought his own paper.

After his host left, the President returned to his writing,

crossing out a word here, substituting another word there—reading and rereading the sentences he had written. At about eleven o'clock, Mr. Lincoln sent for his host again. He would like, he explained, to have a few words with his Secretary of State. Did Mr. Wills know where Mr. Seward could be found?

The Commissioner explained that his next-door neighbor, Mr. Harper, had offered to entertain Mr. Seward. The house was only a few steps away, and he'd be glad to go over and ask the Secretary to come to Mr. Lincoln's room.

Oh no, that wouldn't be necessary, the President explained. He would prefer to go to Mr. Seward's room himself. But would Mr. Wills mind accompanying him to the Harper house?

The President picked up the two sheets of paper upon which he had been writing and followed his host down the stairway. By using the door which faced on the public square, the two men had only a few steps to walk to the Harper residence next door. Sergeant Bigham followed a short distance behind Mr. Lincoln, standing guard at the Harpers' door while the President conferred with Mr. Seward.

It was almost midnight when Mr. Lincoln emerged from Mr. Seward's bedroom. What the two men talked about has never been revealed. But it's a well-known fact that the President placed great value on the advice of his Secretary of State. And it's safe to assume that Mr. Lincoln was asking the opinion of his Secretary about the speech he would make at tomorrow's dedication.

The governor of Pennsylvania, Andrew Curtin, had been invited to the Wills dinner party on that Wednesday evening.

The Lane Studio, Gettysburg, Pa.

The bedroom in Mr. Wills' home, where President Lincoln finished writing his Gettysburg Address. A wax figure of Mr. Lincoln may be seen in the foreground.

His special excursion train from Harrisburg had been scheduled to arrive in plenty of time for the evening's festivities. However, an accident outside Hanover Junction had detained the train for almost five hours. It was nearly eleven-thirty P.M. when the special reached Gettysburg, carrying the Baltimore Glee Club as well as the prominent government officials from Harrisburg.

Now that the members of the Glee Club had reached their destination, they were in no mood to go to bed. The night was yet young and they had missed too much fun already. They decided to hunt up the President and serenade him with their favorite rendition of "We Are Coming, Father Abraham, Three Hundred Thousand More." First published as a poem by James S. Gibbons in the *New York Evening Post*, July 12, 1862, the sentimental phrases and swinging rhythm had captured the imagination of the entire country. The poem was set to music almost immediately and soon became the most popular of all Civil War songs.

While he was still talking to Mr. Seward, the President heard the Baltimore singers outside. But after the fiasco earlier in the evening, Mr. Lincoln was determined to make no speeches. The President simply acknowledged the serenaders with a bow as he came out of the Harper house, and whispered to Sergeant Bigham, "You clear a way, sergeant, and I will hang on to your coat." The young bodyguard was proud of his assignment and eager to provide the best protection possible. Within moments he had Mr. Lincoln safely inside the Wills home.

Governor Curtin had just arrived and was being welcomed by his host. Mr. Lincoln paused only a few moments to greet his good friend, then retired to his room. Soon afterward, Mr. Wills saw William Johnson leaving, so he felt certain that Mr. Lincoln would not be down again this evening.

A few minutes later a telegram arrived for the President. Sergeant Bigham knocked on the bedroom door and handed the message to Mr. Lincoln. Alone in his room, the President opened the missile. It read: "Hon. A. Lincoln, Gettysburg, Pa. The Dr. has just left. We hope dear Taddie is slightly better. Will send you a telegram in the morning. Mrs. Lincoln."

Such news was too good to keep to himself. The President opened the door and told a very surprised sergeant that the telegram he had just received was from home, that his boy was very sick, but now he was better. Then he closed the door and turned out the oil lamp beside his bed. Tomorrow would be a long day, and he must try to get some sleep.

Outside in the public square the confusion had begun to subside. There were still bands playing, still people who were roaming the streets, irrespective of the late hour. But the little town was gradually quieting down to await the big event on Thursday.

FIVE

The Dedication Ceremony

ALL Gettysburg was astir early on this morning of Thursday, November 19. Low-hanging clouds had held a threat of rain when dawn broke. But fortunately they had disappeared, leaving a bright sun and a cloudless blue sky. There was a crisp tang in the air, a kind of crystal-clear atmosphere that brought the surrounding hills into sharp relief.

Roads leading into the town were clogged with carriages, buggies, wagons, and conveyances of every kind. Some families had driven all night. Others had left their homes before dawn in order to reach Gettysburg in time for the dedication. Those who had arrived on Wednesday had had to find overnight lodgings wherever they could. Rooms in the Eagle Hotel had been filled weeks ahead of time. Many residents had opened their homes to the visitors, but the number of arrivals had far exceeded the available beds. Some had slept in church pews or on improvised beds in public buildings. And there were many who hadn't been to bed at all.

Shortly before nine o'clock people began assembling in the public square, ready to take their places in the line of march to the cemetery. Marshal Lamon's instructions had been very specific. The military would form up precisely at nine A.M. on Carlisle Street, north of the square, under the direction of Major General Couch.

The state marshals and Marshal Lamon's aides were to gather in the public square, ready to direct the various groups. Each man had been provided with a bulky yellow and white scarf which was to be worn stretched over the right shoulder and under the left arm, so the crowd would have no trouble in identifying these officials.

Representatives of various civic groups were to be on York Street, while the delegation of Pennsylvania citizens would form up on Chambersburg Street, followed by citizens' groups from other states. Furthermore, Lamon had instructed each marshal to direct his delegation so it would take its proper place when the procession began to move.

Four bands had come to Gettysburg to take part in the procession: the United States Marine Band from Washington, Baltimore's Second United States Artillery Band, Philadelphia's Birgfield Band, and the band of the Fifth New York Heavy Artillery. Now Marshal Lamon was having some problems, trying to place the bands at intervals in the parade so they would not drown each other out.

Inside the Wills' home, the overnight guests were finishing breakfast. Mr. Lincoln arose from the table rather abruptly, saying that he must return to his room and do some work before the parade began. John Nicolay, the President's secretary, went to Mr. Lincoln's room at about nine o'clock to report for duty and found the President writing at the improvised desk, oblivious to the noisy confusion outside his window in the public square.

William, the valet, moved quietly about the room, getting out the President's long white gauntlets, brushing the black Prince Albert coat, straightening the mourning band on the tall stovepipe hat which the President would wear. He still insisted on that black band to honor the memory of his son Willie. The President ignored the valet's actions.

When Mr. Lincoln had finished, he folded up the two sheets of paper and put them into his pocket. Precisely at ten o'clock he emerged from the Wills house on the York Street side. A small group of soldiers had lined up on either side of the door, forming a pathway for the President as he walked out to mount his waiting horse, a "magnificent chestnut bay" furnished by Adam Rebert, a Gettysburg resident. Many people said that even this horse wasn't large enough for the President's long legs. His feet almost touched the ground as he sat astride the animal.

Rounds of cheers for the President rang out and people began crowding in around the horse in order to shake Mr. Lincoln's hand. The President was forced to hold an informal reception for almost an hour. While he was greeting the people, a telegram was handed him from Secretary of War Stanton. The careworn face brightened visibly as he read: "Mrs. Lincoln reports your son's health a great deal better and he will be out today."

During the long wait, some of the marchers decided they

would prefer to go on out to the cemetery in order to get a better vantage point. When the procession finally began to move at eleven A.M., it was somewhat reduced in size. Nevertheless, it was still an impressive sight.

The military led off with Major General Couch in command. Next came the Fifth New York Heavy Artillery Band. Behind them rode the President with Secretary Seward and Postmaster-General Blair on his right. Marshal Lamon and Secretary Usher flanked the President on the left. John Hay and John Nicolay followed behind with ranking officials, governors, and mayors. Bringing up the rear were the various civic organizations and citizens from a number of northern states.

The presidential procession began moving out from the public square past the tall flagpole with its flag at half-mast. Governor Curtin had ordered that all flags should be flown at half-mast on this day of dedication. As the parade turned onto Baltimore Street, Mr. Lincoln caught sight of an eager father holding his tiny daughter high in his arms. The President halted the march momentarily and reached down to take the little girl. For a moment she sat astride the President's horse with him. Then kissing her on the forehead, Mr. Lincoln handed her back to the happy father. The watching crowd cheered.

The parade route had been carefully laid out by Marshal Lamon. They marched up Baltimore Street to the Emmitsburg Road, then to the junction of the Taneytown Road and on out to the cemetery. The bands took turns blaring out their martial music. Every sixty seconds a battery of guns was fired. To the Cincinnati *Daily Gazette* reporter, it sounded like "the roar of battle, reverberating from the hills and mountains."

Lieutenant Cochrane, who was riding behind the President, later recalled that Mr. Lincoln sat his mount with ease, "bowing occasionally to right and left." He also noted that Secretary Seward was having some difficulty with his trousers. They kept working up over his shoes, as he rode, revealing his homemade gray knit socks.

As the procession proceeded along the dirt street, Mr. Lincoln could not fail to see the devastating evidence of the three-day battle in July. The once-trim white wooden fences were now splintered and full of holes from stray rifle bullets. Solid shot could be seen embedded in brick walls. Trees had been broken, their branches still sprawling on the ground. Many homes along the line of march were draped in mourning, silent evidence of the summer's sorrow.

At first the President sat erect and straight in the saddle, but as the procession moved further along, Mr. Lincoln seemed to become absorbed in his own thoughts. Colonel Carr, the commissioner from Illinois, was riding behind the President. Years later he recalled that before the procession reached the cemetery, the President seemed to slump forward in his saddle, arms dangling at his sides and body "swaying from side to side." This was the position the young Illinois lawyer had assumed as he rode the long circuit trail during his early years of law practice. Today he seemed to have slipped back into a habit established long ago.

The parade route was short, actually about half a mile in length. By eleven-fifteen A.M. the military escort was lined up around the wooden platform which had been temporarily

The Library of Congress

The procession moving out on Baltimore Street toward the cemetery on the morning of November 19, 1863.

erected for the ceremony. Rising only three feet above the ground, the platform was hardly adequate for the number of dignitaries who would be seated on it. Such a low platform made it difficult, too, for the audience to see much of what was going on. Bunting had been draped around it, though the flag on the pole had not been lowered to half-mast. Someone had forgotten that detail!

All work of reburying the soldiers had been suspended for the day, but the pine boxes and the freshly dug graves were tangible evidence that the work had begun. Actually, the transferral had started late in October and by November 19th, 1,188 Union soldiers had been reburied, at a cost of $1.59 a body. There had been thirty-four bids submitted to the Board of Commissioners, all the way from $8 to $1.59. But the board had chosen the lowest bidder.

When the President arrived, the soldiers snapped to attention and every man in the audience took off his hat as Mr. Lincoln acknowledged the military salute. The platform was crowded with dignitaries: the governors of the states participating in the cemetery, cabinet members, and military officials. The President was escorted to an "old dingy uncushioned settee" as the Cincinnati *Daily Gazette* reporter described it. Secretary Seward would sit on the President's left with Mr. Everett on his right. However, the orator of the day had not yet put in his appearance.

Mr. Lincoln said little to Secretary Seward while they sat waiting for Mr. Everett. The President was probably recalling those three terrible days in July as he gazed out over the landscape. To his left was Cemetery Hill and on beyond were the wooded areas that sloped gently into Culp's Hill. On the right was Seminary Ridge, where the Confederate lines had been assembled. Far to the south were Big and Little Round Tops, the rocky expanse of Devil's Den, the Valley of Death, and the Wheatfield—names now familiar only because of the intensive fighting on July 1st, 2nd, and 3rd. Straight ahead was the broken stone wall at the Bloody Angle where determined Union soldiers had heaped their dead in order that Pickett's brigade would not break through.

Mr. Wills had promised to deliver Mr. Everett in plenty of time but no one seemed to know where they were. As the minutes passed, the dignitaries on the platform began craning their necks, trying to locate the missing speaker. The bands were doing their best to keep everyone entertained, though the thousands who were standing on the battlefield began to get somewhat restless. What in the world was holding up the ceremony?

It was noon when Mr. Wills hustled up to the platform with Mr. Everett. The orator had been taking a final look at the battlefield. He was sorry, time had just slipped away. And the proceedings began, one hour behind schedule.

The dedication ceremony opened with a dirge played by the Birgfield Band. Then the Rev. Dr. T.H. Stockton, chaplain of the United States House of Representatives, arose to pronounce the invocation. Although somewhat lengthy, the prayer stirred many memories for the audience. A reporter from the *Philadelphia Press* noted that there were tears on the cheeks of both the President and Mr. Everett.

After the Marine Band had played "Old Hundred," Benjamin B. French, Officer in Charge of Buildings in Washington, introduced the orator of the day, "The Honorable Edward Everett."

Arising from the settee, Mr. Everett turned to Mr. Lin-

The Library of Congress

The cemetery gate at Gettysburg as it was photographed in 1863.

The Library of Congress

Part of the great crowd that had assembled awaiting the beginning of the dedication ceremony.

coln with a courtly bow, saying, "Mr. President." The President responded with "Mr. Everett," whereupon the speaker stepped to the center of the platform. He stood for a moment looking out over the vast audience and toward the hills beyond, an impressive man with long white hair, erect as a ramrod in his well-cut, black suit coat with a high white collar and long, flowing, black tie.

"Standing beneath this serene sky," he began, and proceeded to describe the scene about him. Then, "It is with hesitation that I raise my poor voice to break the eloquent silence of God and Nature." But Mr. Everett was an orator of the old school. He had made extensive preparation and this was his greatest moment. His gestures were faultless as he carried his audience from the cemetery prepared for Greek heroes through a detailed account of the three days of fighting.

An hour had passed and most people thought that surely Mr. Everett was almost finished. But he continued for another hour, urging reconciliation between the North and South, finally bringing his oration to a triumphant close with the words: "In the glorious annals of our common country, there will be no brighter page than that which relates the Battles of Gettysburg."

During the two-hour speech, Mr. Lincoln listened intently to the orator. He was fascinated by the gentleman's performance. The fact that Mr. Everett had memorized his entire speech, that he could speak for two solid hours without once referring to his notes, was a feat that impressed the President as well as the audience. There were those, however, who could not hear the rather high voice of the speaker, and they began wandering away to pick up whatever souvenirs they could find on the battlefield: a bullet, a torn piece of uniform, a discarded knapsack.

"Thundering applause" rang out as Mr. Everett took his seat after the speech, a speech which one reporter compared to a piece of Greek sculpture, "beautiful, but cold as ice." Mr. Lincoln was quick to offer his congratulations to the perspiring orator.

The Baltimore Glee Club now arose to sing the hymn which Benjamin French had composed and given to Mr. Wills three weeks before. The director used a small American flag as his baton (and later presented it to Agnes McCleary, the young daughter of his Gettysburg host). During the singing Mr. Lincoln took out his steel-bowed glasses and adjusted them over his ears. Then he pulled out two sheets of paper from his pocket and glanced at them hastily. When the hymn was finished, Marshal Ward Hill Lamon arose and introduced his old friend, "The President of the United States."

Mr. Lincoln pulled himself up slowly from the settee and stepped to the front of the bunting-draped platform. Behind him were the freshly dug graves of the soldiers who had fallen in the Battle of Gettysburg. In front were the Honor Guard soldiers with their bayonets glinting in the autumn sun, and beyond—a sea of faces waiting expectantly for the President's remarks.

Interspersed in the crowd were soldiers in faded blue uniforms, some on crutches, others with empty sleeves. This was the first opportunity many of the visitors had had to get a good look at Mr. Lincoln, and there was some confusion as people shuffled around for a better view.

The President stood silent for a moment, his head bowed

as he waited for the crowd to quiet down. When he lifted his face, people saw the haggard, heavy lines, the deep-set gray eyes that seemed so sad, yet somehow hopeful. In a ringing, high-pitched voice he began, "Fourscore and seven years ago . . ."

Mr. Lincoln spoke slowly, enunciating each word with deliberate precision. People noticed the slight Kentucky twang of his early childhood. His voice seemed to have a thin, metallic sound. Yet it was a voice that carried well, one that could be heard in large crowds. He used no gestures, and referred only once to the papers which he held in his hand.

When the President came to the words, "The world will little note nor long remember what we say here, but it can never forget what they did here. . . ." his voice quivered and almost broke. But he recovered himself quickly. And in a few moments the audience heard his final phrase, ". . . that this nation, under God, shall have a new birth of freedom —and that government of the people, by the people, for the people shall not perish from the earth."

The entire address had lasted little more than two minutes. At one edge of the platform photographer Alexander Gardner was still trying to get his camera in focus when the President sat down. John Russell Young, a Philadelphia reporter, leaned over to Mr. Lincoln and asked if that was all. The President replied, "Yes, for the present."

There was little, if any, applause; the audience was too dazed. They hadn't expected a great deal, but surely the President of the United States should have said more than he did. They hadn't even settled down to listen before the speech was over.

The Library of Congress

The Honorable Edward Everett, main speaker at the dedication ceremony in Gettysburg, November 19, 1863.

Mr. Lincoln was a very perceptive person. He could feel the disappointment of his audience. He turned to his friend, Marshal Lamon, on the platform and said, "Lamon, that speech won't scour. It is a flat failure and the people are disappointed." (The word "scour" was an idiom sometimes used by the early Illinois farmers. When wet soil stuck to the moldboard of a rusty plow, the farmer said it wouldn't "scour," meaning that it was not working smoothly.)

After the choir had sung, "Oh! It is Great for our Country to Die!" the Rev. H.L. Baugher, president of Gettysburg College, pronounced the benediction and the official ceremony was over. Now the dignitaries were moving off the platform. Marshal Lamon overheard Mr. Everett asking Mr. Seward what he thought of the President's speech. The Secretary of State replied, "He has made a failure and I am sorry for it."

SIX

Later That Afternoon

NOW the military escort was forming up, ready to precede the President back to the David Wills home. Mr. Lincoln mounted his waiting horse and, with Marshal Lamon at his side, rode back into town.

Scattered remnants of the procession followed, but the states' marshals were making no attempt to organize their marching units. Many people had run out ahead of the escort, taking up positions along the Taneytown Road and Baltimore Street in order to wave as the President rode by. The solemnity of the occasion seemed to have permeated through the crowds. Boisterous cheering had given way to respectful silence.

The luncheon had been long delayed. No one had

dreamed that Mr. Everett would talk for two hours, least of all, Mrs. Wills. Nevertheless, she concealed her agitation when her guests sat down at the table shortly after three o'clock.

Someone mentioned Gettysburg's only civilian volunteer during the battle, seventy-year-old John Burns. Mr. Lincoln was very much interested. Burns, he was told, was quite a character, reportedly only five feet tall and a veteran of the War of 1812. When he came to Gettysburg, he was the village cobbler, and later he was elected constable. This was an office which the old man took very seriously, feeling that it was his solemn duty to preserve peace in the community, whatever the cost.

On the morning of July 1st, John Burns heard that the Confederates were approaching from the north by way of the Chambersburg Road. Without a moment's hesitation, he stuffed his pockets with homemade bullets, slung his old-fashioned powder horn over his shoulder, grabbed up his flintlock squirrel rifle, and started out to put down the rebellion for his town.

Old John attached himself to the One-Hundred-and-Fiftieth Pennsylvania Volunteers. A few soldiers smiled at the ancient squirrel hunter, but they were impressed with his apparent vigor. The Volunteers were holding the hill between McPherson's barn and the adjacent woods, fighting in the open. When they fell back to the ridge, old John moved over to the Iron Brigade. These men were mainly attempting to hold the woods against the attacking Confederates, superior in number. When the Iron Brigade was forced to retreat, the old constable stood his ground beside a tree. A sure shot with his trusty squirrel rifle, he continued picking off Confederate cavalrymen until he was wounded three times.

Captured by the enemy, the old man was left for dead among the many fallen soldiers. He lay on the ground all night until someone found him, still alive, the following morning. The wounds had healed now, Mr. Lincoln was told, and old John was still around to talk about his fighting days. The President expressed an interest in meeting the patriotic old soldier. Mr. Wills said that he would try to arrange it.

As soon as the luncheon was finished, Mr. Lincoln's host explained that there were still people who wanted to shake the President's hand. If Mr. Lincoln didn't object, they would hold a sort of public reception. Would Mr. Lincoln mind standing near the door on the York Street side? People could come in that door, shake hands with the President, and move on into Mr. Wills' private office to meet the friendly Pennsylvania governor before making their exit through the door which faced on the public square.

No, Mr. Lincoln had no objections. He was used to these public receptions, or levees (as they were often called). For an hour the people streamed through the house. Mr. Lincoln's mind seemed to be far away as he shook hands in a mechanical fashion. Occasionally the sad face would light up as a small boy or girl came through the line. And once, a very tall man approached. The President stopped him and asked him what his exact height was; he always liked to compare notes with unusually tall men.

A few minutes before five, Mr. Wills introduced old John Burns to Mr. Lincoln. The constable had been summoned to the Wills residence and he proudly appeared in his "battle dress," a high-crowned felt hat and long blue coat which still had the bullet holes in the back. The President greeted old John with unusual warmth.

But now they had to hurry off to a patriotic meeting which Mr. Wills had arranged for five o'clock. It was to be held in the Presbyterian Church just down the street. Mr. Wills was an elder and had no problem arranging the meeting to be held there. Colonel Anderson, lieutenant-governor-elect of Ohio, would make the address.

Mr. Lincoln invited John Burns to attend the service with him. People smiled with amusement as the very tall President and the unusually short constable walked together down Baltimore Street—the one taking his usual long strides and the other trying to keep pace. Upon entering the church, they were shown to seats in the second pew. (Today, visitors identify the pew by two tablets there. One reads: "Abraham Lincoln sat in this pew at a patriotic service held on the evening he dedicated the National Cemetery." The other tablet says: "John Burns, Scottish-American patriot. A hero of the Battle of Gettysburg was here signally honored by the great President. Abraham Lincoln and John Burns walked arm in arm to patriotic services in this edifice on the evening of November 19, 1863. They sat together in this pew.")

The patriotic meeting lasted longer than anyone expected. Before Colonel Anderson had finished his vitriolic speech about vengeance for the slain soldiers, Mr. Lincoln realized that he would have to leave. His train was scheduled to depart at six-fifteen P.M. He whispered good-by to his companion and made his way down the aisle. People stretched

The Library of Congress

Old John Burns, photographed in the clothes he wore during the Battle of Gettysburg.

out their hands for a final farewell as he walked toward the back of the church.

The Carlisle Street Station was crowded when the President arrived. Many travelers were trying to get passage on one of the various trains scheduled for departure after the Presidential Special left. (An official order had been given that no train was to leave ahead of the Special. Accidents on the rail lines were all too frequent. They couldn't take any chances with the President of the United States aboard.) Hundreds of Mr. Lincoln's well-wishers had crowded onto the platform too. Marshal Lamon had difficulty clearing a pathway.

A few moments after Mr. Lincoln entered the rear car, the train began moving slowly out of the station. The President stepped out on the rear platform and waved farewell to the people and to the little town of Gettysburg, a town whose name would become known all over the world because of the "few appropriate remarks" he had made on this day of November 19, 1863.

Representative Wayne MacVeagh was riding the Special only as far as Hanover Junction. He made his way back to the rear car and asked if Mr. Lincoln would have a little time to talk with him. After discussing politics for a while, Mr. MacVeagh turned the conversation to the afternoon's ceremonies, saying, "The words you spoke, Mr. President, will live in the land's language."

The President thought MacVeagh was very extravagant with his praise and told him so. "You are the only person," he affirmed, "who has such a misconception of what I said."

After MacVeagh left the compartment, Mr. Lincoln real-

The Lane Studio, Gettysburg, Pa.

The pew occupied by President Lincoln during a patriotic service at the Presbyterian Church in Gettysburg, late in the afternoon on November 19, 1863.

ized how tired he was. A dull headache had set his temples throbbing. He asked William to put some chairs together so that he might lie down. The resourceful valet also brought a wet towel to put on the President's forehead. Mr. Lincoln felt hot and feverish but decided it was probably the aftermath of a long and busy day.

It was well after midnight before the Presidential Special reached Washington. Marshal Lamon hurried Mr. Lincoln into the waiting carriage and urged the driver to lose no time in getting them back to the White House. The President looked so tired and worn, Lamon thought. But then it had been a strenuous trip.

Back in Gettysburg, trains were pulling out every few minutes, loaded with people who had to get back to their homes in New York, Baltimore, Philadelphia, and Pittsburgh. Those who had come by wagon or buggy were now driving through the surrounding countryside over roads that, fortunately, were still firm, not yet muddy or rutted by a late autumn freeze.

When the people who had been to Gettysburg arrived home, they lost no time in telling their neighbors about the bands, the procession, and the dedication ceremony. Yes, Mr. Everett had made a speech, a very long one, in fact. And they had seen Mr. Lincoln. And—oh yes, he had made a few remarks. His speech was so short, though—he certainly hadn't said much. But they were glad they had seen him, anyway. Maybe he wasn't much to look at, but he had the kindest face in the world.

SEVEN

The Press Reports

THE little community of Gettysburg did not have the telegraph facilities of a metropolitan area. There were few telegraph offices, and many reporters who had been sent to cover the dedication ceremony had difficulty getting their stories on the wire.

Orator Edward Everett had anticipated this difficulty ahead of time. An entry in his diary for Saturday, November 14, says that he had sent a copy of his manuscript to the Boston *Daily Advertiser* to be set in type and that he was pleased with the proofs which he had just received. Once the story was set in type, it was released to all the leading newspapers throughout the country, ready for publication with the reporters' stories of the dedication.

A short "release" was wired from Gettysburg early on the morning of November 19. The story merely stated that the weather was fine and the program would be carried out as planned. Local color was added by detailing the events of the preceding night including the serenading parties and the speeches by the various dignitaries. In one or two papers, the President's little speech on Mr. Wills' porch was mistakenly printed as, "The President's Address." This was the exception, however. Most papers received their reports in plenty of time for the morning issues of November 20.

Among the reporters present at the ceremony was Joseph L. Gilbert of the Associated Press. Standing on the ground directly in front of the President as he spoke, reporter Gilbert began taking the address down in shorthand. However, he stopped when he saw the papers in Mr. Lincoln's hand. And immediately after the President was finished, the reporter asked to borrow the manuscript so that he might complete his report. It was Gilbert's Associated Press version of Mr. Lincoln's remarks that was published the following day in many leading newspapers across the country. Variations occur in the text but these were probably due to mistakes made by telegraph operators and the men at the newspaper offices who transcribed the telegrams.

A more complete shorthand report was made by Charles Hale, nephew of the orator Edward Everett. Mr. Hale was present at the ceremony as a representative of Massachusetts. But he was also acting as a correspondent for the Boston *Daily Advertiser*. His story, which appeared on Friday, November 20, 1863, is believed to be one of the most authentic of all news reports.

The story of the happenings at Gettysburg had much competition in the *New York Times* of November 20. Burnside's movements around Knoxville were covered by a full column on the left hand side of the front page. It was war news that sold papers. People wanted even the smallest details.

Then there was the Delaware election which had to be reported. And the controversial Henry Ward Beecher, who had just returned from England, had delivered a lengthy speech in New York City. This was important enough to command three front-page columns. Sandwiched between the war news and the Rev. Beecher was a story captioned "The Heroes of July," a one-and-a-half-column article on the dedication at Gettysburg. The President's speech was reprinted, but there was no editorial comment on his remarks.

The *New York Tribune* newsman quoted the President's speech with one short introductory sentence: "The dedicatory remarks were then delivered by the President." But the *New York Herald* man merely mentioned that Mr. Lincoln had said a few words. He didn't even bother to report the speech.

An unknown reporter for the *Chicago Tribune* is credited with the first favorable comment on the President's address. Filing a short story from Gettysburg on the evening of November 19—the story which appeared in the *Tribune* on November 20—he gave the order of events and ended with: "The oration by Hon. Edward Everett, the solemn dirge by the choir, and the dedication remarks by President Lincoln will live among the annals of the war."

The following day the *Chicago Tribune* reporter filed a second story from Harrisburg, explaining that his Gettysburg story had been necessarily brief because of the inadequate telegraph facilities. This longer story called the dedication ceremony "the most impressive civic occasion of the war." The reporter finished his story with this comment: "More than any other single event will this glorious dedication serve the heroism, and deepen the resolution of the living to conquer at all hazards. More than anything else will this day's work contribute to the nationality of the great republic."

Unlike the presidents who had preceded him, Mr. Lincoln was completely at the mercy of the press. Ever since the days of Thomas Jefferson, the chief executive had released his news and views only to certain "pet newspapers" or "organs," as they were sometimes called. These papers were edited, directly or indirectly, by the president's political supporters and reflected only the views which the chief executive favored.

Mr. Lincoln broke with this long-established policy by refusing to have an "official" outlet for news. Historians today believe that the Civil War President declined to show favoritism because he wanted to secure as much support as possible from both Democratic and Republican newspapers.

Although the formal news conference was still an event of the future, President Lincoln welcomed reporters at almost any hour. He liked to chat with them informally, usually asking more questions than he answered. Gideon Welles, Secretary of the Navy, deplored this practice, noting in his diary: "It is an infirmity of the President that he permits the little newsmongers to come around him and be intimate. He has great inquisitiveness. Likes to hear all the political gossip . . ." However, it was more than "political gossip" that Mr. Lincoln wanted. Through the newsmen, he felt that he was keeping in touch with the "popular masses."

William O. Stoddard, one of the President's secretaries, believed that Mr. Lincoln learned much from his contact with the reporters. In writing about these newsmen, Mr. Stoddard said, "Probably they have no idea how much they tell him. As if through so many human magnetic wires, he receives message after message from the current thought and purpose of the popular masses whom he understands so much better than they do."

Despite the President's efforts, many newspapers of that day were violently anti-Lincoln. And the Gettysburg speech made an excellent target for their acrid commentaries. Some even proclaimed that he had "desecrated the graves of Union soldiers" by making what they termed "a political speech" in the National Cemetery. The *Patriot and Union* of Harrisburg, Pennsylvania, said: "We pass over the silly remarks of the President; for the credit of the nation we are willing that the veil of oblivion shall be dropped over them and that they shall no more be repeated or thought of."

The *Chicago Times* had only caustic comments to make about Mr. Lincoln's address: "The cheek of every American must tingle with shame as he reads the silly, flat and dish-watery utterances of the man who has to be pointed out to intelligent foreigners as the President of the United States." And when the pro-Confederate paper, the *Richmond Examiner*, editorialized that "On the present occasion Lincoln acted like a clown," the *Chicago Times* reprinted the entire editorial.

On the whole, however, the northern editors gave the Gettysburg Address good reviews. The Springfield, Massachusetts, *Republican* called it "a perfect gem, deep in feeling, compact in thought and expression."

The editor of the *Providence Journal* explained to his readers that making a short speech is one of the most difficult tasks in the world and added, "We know not where to look for a more admirable speech than the brief one which the President made at the close of Mr. Everett's oration. . . . Could the most elaborate and splendid oration be more beautiful, more touching, more inspiring than those thrilling words of the President? They had in our humble judgment the charm and power of the very highest eloquence."

Praise came, too, from the Philadelphia *Evening Bulletin*: "The President's brief speech of dedication is most happily expressed. It is warm, earnest, unaffected, and touching. Thousands who would not read the long, elaborate oration of Mr. Everett will read the President's few words, and not many will do it without a moistening of the eye and a swelling of the heart."

On Monday, November 23rd, the editor of the Detroit *Advertiser and Tribune* made the Gettysburg ceremony the subject of his lead editorial. He wrote that Mr. Everett had delivered an "extended and elaborate oration" about the three heroic days in July. Then he added, "But he who wants to take in the very spirit of the day, catch the unstudied pathos that animates a sincere but very simple-minded man, will turn from the stately periods of the professed orator to the brief speech of the President."

Strangely enough, the *Washington Chronicle* had several

correspondents at the dedication ceremony but in the November 20 edition, nothing was said about the President's speech. However, on the following day a sixteen-page pamphlet was issued, entitled, "The Gettysburg Solemnities." Mr. Lincoln's remarks were reprinted on the last page.

News of the dedication traveled across the Atlantic, but comment was anything but complimentary. The December 4th issue of the *London Times* told its readers that: "The ceremony was rendered ludicrous by some of the sallies of that poor President Lincoln. . . . Anything more dull and commonplace would not be easy to produce."

In contrast to the English opinion was the praise given by George William Curtis, editor of *Harper's Weekly*, the leading American magazine of that time. In the issue of December 5, 1863, Mr. Curtis wrote: "The oration by Mr. Everett was smooth and cold. Delivered doubtless with his accustomed graces, it yet wanted one stirring thought, one vivid picture, one thrilling appeal. The few words of the President were from the heart to the heart. They cannot be read, even, without kindling emotion."

Editor Curtis accorded even higher praise in the issue of April 23, 1864. Writing about the President's address, he called it "the most perfect piece of American eloquence, and as noble and pathetic and appropriate as the oration of Pericles over the Peloponnesian dead."

In his remarks at the dedication ceremony President Lincoln had not attempted to deliver an oration. He had been instructed to keep his remarks short and he probably realized that the occasion was too solemn for anything but a few simple sentences. He made no attempt to "carry his audience" with him, as he had done in the old Illinois days of campaign oratory.

Because Mr. Lincoln's address was so brief, it is not hard to understand why the reporters who heard him speak did not consciously appreciate what they had heard—why many of them merely wrote that the President also made a few remarks.

It was, therefore, as literature rather than oratory that the address was to be judged. Newspaper editors read and reread the few short sentences before making editorial comment. And today, it is as a fine piece of writing that the world knows the Gettysburg Address, not as a great oration.

EIGHT

In the Weeks After

MR. LINCOLN had thought that he was only very very tired after the strenuous two days in Gettysburg, that his throbbing headache on the train trip home was just a temporary reaction to seeing so many people, shaking so many hands.

When the early morning sun streamed into the windows of his White House bedroom on that Friday morning, November 20th, the President knew that something more serious was wrong. The fever hadn't diminished. He ached all over. His body felt hot and dry as he tossed and turned in the huge eight-foot bed. Tad ran in shouting, "Papa-Day, Papa-Day" and made a leap for his father's long bony frame. Even this joyous greeting failed to arouse the President for

National Park Service

Mr. Lincoln's oversized bed, now in the Lincoln bedroom of the White House.

the accustomed romp. He could only stroke the little fellow's hair.

And there were so many things to be done. Congress was convening in less than three weeks and his message was still not finished. Then there was the Amnesty Proclamation which he wanted to complete. This was a project very dear to the President's heart; it was to be the beginning of reconciliation with the South. He wanted to guarantee a full pardon to all southern soldiers who would take an oath of loyalty to the United States Constitution and swear to uphold the Emancipation Proclamation. There was still much work to be done before he could submit his idea to Congress.

The doctor diagnosed Mr. Lincoln's illness as a "varioloid," a mild form of smallpox. It was not too surprising. The disease had reached almost epidemic proportions in the city of Washington during that fall of 1863. The President was relieved that his case was not one of the more serious ones. He laughingly said that he now had something he could give everyone.

During that Friday morning "an intelligent woman in deep distress" called at the White House. Although he was miserable, Mr. Lincoln insisted on getting out of bed to see his caller. Her husband, she explained, was sentenced to be shot next Monday. Couldn't the President do something?

A message was put on the wire immediately. "If there is a man by the name of King under sentence to be shot, please suspend execution till further order, and send record."

After his caller had left, Mr. Lincoln discovered that the information in the letter she had given him was not definite. She had signed her name as "Mrs. Anna S. King" and had said her husband was a lieutenant. But she had supplied neither his first name nor the number of his regiment.

Mr. Lincoln couldn't get the anxious woman's face out of his mind. Perhaps the wire to General Meade had not given sufficient detail. He got out of bed and sent another message, a more lengthy one giving all the particulars of the case in order to be sure that the man would not be shot.

During that Friday afternoon, a letter arrived at the White House from 225 H Street, Washington. Edward Everett was writing to thank the President for the kindnesses which he had shown Mr. Everett's daughter, Mrs. Wise, on the trip to Gettysburg. Further, the orator wrote: "I should be glad, if I could flatter myself that I came as near to the central idea of the occasion, in two hours, as you did in two minutes."

Mr. Lincoln replied immediately: "Your kind note of today is received. In our respective parts yesterday, you could not have been excused to make a short address, nor I a long one. I am pleased to know that, in your judgment, the little I did say was not entirely a failure."

Edward Everett's generous compliment revived the President's sagging spirits about his speech at Gettysburg. Perhaps the few remarks hadn't been such a failure, after all. When his old friend, the Honorable James Speed, called at the White House a few days later, Mr. Lincoln showed him the letter from Mr. Everett. Mr. Speed later recalled that the President was very pleased and said that he had "never received a compliment he prized more highly."

On November 23, Mr. Lincoln received a letter from Commissioner Wills, his host at Gettysburg. In behalf of the governors, Mr. Wills asked that the President send the "original manuscript" of his speech at the dedication so that it could be filed with all the papers connected with the project.

Mr. Lincoln did not send the "original manuscript." Historians differ on whether he actually sent a copy of the address in his own handwriting. If he did, it is not in existence today. It is believed that the President did not think that the first draft of his remarks was good enough to send to Mr. Wills. Directing his secretaries to make copies of the Associated Press reports of the speech as it had been printed in various newspapers, Mr. Lincoln made a few changes and corrections in the margins. It is probable that since he was still sick in bed, one of the secretaries recopied the address with the suggested changes and sent it along to David Wills. The version of the address as it was printed in the official Gettysburg volume of the proceedings does not agree completely with the final version which we know today.

Late in January, 1864, the President had another communication from Mr. Everett. In New York City, the orator explained, a large Metropolitan Fair was planned for April, 1864—a fair which would be held for the benefit of the Civil War soldiers. Mrs. Hamilton Fish was chairman of the Ladies' Committee. It was her idea to procure the manuscripts of Mr. Everett's oration and Mr. Lincoln's address and have them bound together to be sold at the fair. Would Mr. Lincoln agree to this, Mr. Everett wanted to know?

The President was always sympathetic to any cause which benefited his fighting men. Nothing, he felt, was too much trouble if in any way it helped even one soldier. He carefully recopied his "few remarks" and on February 4, 1864, wrote Mr. Everett: "I am sending herewith the manuscript of my remarks at Gettysburg."

At a reception in the White House on February 23, 1864, the famous historian, George Bancroft, was present. He managed to see Mr. Lincoln alone for a few moments. The City of Baltimore, he explained, was staging a Sanitary Fair this spring, a fair similar to the one in New York City, to benefit sick soldiers. One of the committees was collecting famous manuscripts which they wanted to have lithographed and sold as a volume called, *Autograph Leaves of Our Country's Authors*. Mr. Bancroft's stepson, Colonel Alexander Bliss, was a member of that committee and had commissioned Mr. Bancroft to ask the President for a handwritten copy of the Gettysburg Address. Would Mr. Lincoln be willing to make such a copy?

The President agreed that he would be more than happy to make such a copy. Sometime within the next few days he found time to recopy his "few appropriate remarks," writing on both sides of a single sheet of paper. In dispatching the speech to George Bancroft on February 29, 1864, Mr. Lincoln wrote: "Herewith is the copy of the manuscript which you did me the honor to request."

John P. Kennedy of Baltimore had been assigned the task of editing the proposed *Autograph Leaves*. When Mr. Lincoln's handwritten manuscript reached the editor's desk, Mr. Kennedy was very disturbed. With writing on both sides of a single sheet, the manuscript could not be lithographed properly for publication. Besides, there should be a heading on it, and Mr. Lincoln's signature was needed.

Mr. Kennedy wrote the White House, asking if the President would "appropriate another quarter-hour to the making of another copy." Mr. Lincoln's secretary, John Nicolay, answered that another copy would be forthcoming if the instructions could be more specific. Perhaps even a sheet of paper could be enclosed which would indicate the size and width of margins needed.

Colonel Bliss sent Mr. Nicolay the paper that was requested and also returned the President's manuscript "with great regret." He explained that he had promised to give this copy to his stepfather, George Bancroft, after the publisher had finished with it. Could it possibly be returned with the new copy so as not to disappoint Mr. Bancroft?

Again the President made a copy of his Gettysburg Address, the last known copy ever made in Mr. Lincoln's handwriting. Following the editorial instructions given him, Mr. Lincoln wrote on three sheets of paper and added the heading, "Address delivered at the dedication of the Cemetery at Gettysburg." This is the only copy to which he added his signature.

The copy which Colonel Bliss had requested for his stepfather and the new copy written for the book reached the editor's desk on March 11, 1864. Mr. Lincoln's address was the second entry in the published volume; it followed "The Star Spangled Banner."

As the war problems continued, it is probable that the President had little time to think of those "few remarks" he had made back in November. Nevertheless, with all the requests he had had for autograph copies, it is quite certain that now, at least, he began to realize that he had not failed completely in his address at the Gettysburg National Cemetery.

NINE

The Various Manuscripts

TODAY there are five existing copies of the Gettysburg Address in Mr. Lincoln's own handwriting. The earliest known version is called "The Nicolay Copy," or "First Draft." The first page of this copy is written in ink on stationery which is inscribed, "Executive Mansion." This was undoubtedly written by Mr. Lincoln before he left Washington on November 18 to travel to Gettysburg. Because the first page ends with an incomplete sentence, historians believe that there was probably a second page which the President either destroyed or inadvertently left at the White House.

On the evening of November 18, the President excused himself after dinner at the Wills home, saying that he must go to his room to continue working on the remarks he intended to make. The second page of this First Draft is written in pencil on wide-lined paper, the kind Mr. Lincoln habitually used in drafting public documents.

It is believed that he finished writing the speech either Wednesday evening or after breakfast on Thursday morning. Because there are slight crease marks (indicating a folding of these papers) in the First Draft, the most reliable authorities point out that this is the copy which Mr. Lincoln held in his hand while giving his address at the National Cemetery.

Afterwards, Mr. Lincoln gave this copy to his secretary, John Nicolay. It remained with Mr. Nicolay's private papers until after his death in 1901, when it was given to John Hay.

The "Second Draft," or the "Hay Copy" is the manuscript which is the most difficult to explain. It is written completely in ink on two pages, and the paper is identical to that used for the second page of the First Draft. Some historians believe that this is the copy made in Gettysburg and the one which the President used at the National Cemetery. However, there are no crease marks on these papers, and we do know that Mr. Lincoln folded his speech and carried it in his pocket on the ride to the Cemetery. A more logical explanation of the Second Draft is that Mr. Lincoln probably wrote this one soon after his return to Washington and gave it to his assistant secretary, John Hay.

The First Draft and the Second Draft remained in the papers of John Hay for a number of years. Mr. Hay was named ambassador to Great Britain in 1897 by President McKinley and served as Secretary of State from 1898 until his death in 1905. The widow, Mrs. Hay, once refused an offer of $50,000 for one of the copies. And in 1916 the Hay children, Clarence L., Helen Whitney, and Alice Wadsworth gave both the First Draft and the Second Draft to the Library of Congress, where they may be seen today.

Only once have these two copies been taken out of the Library of Congress. In 1947 Attorney-General Tom Clark conceived the idea of a Freedom Train which would display America's most important historical documents. On September 17 of that year, the red, white, and blue train composed of seven cars was dedicated in Philadelphia. The following day it started out on a 33,000-mile tour. A detachment of marines guarded the precious cargo of one-hundred-and-twenty-eight documents. Three-hundred communities were visited by the Freedom Train during its year-long tour. Thousands of people pored over the historical documents at every stop.

The third known copy of the Gettysburg Address is the one which Edward Everett requested from Mr. Lincoln to be sold at the Metropolitan Fair in New York City. The manuscripts which were bound together were eventually acquired by Carlos Pierce, a railroad magnate from Boston. This is known as the "Everett Copy." After Mr. Pierce died in 1870, his widow kept the manuscripts for some years. Then in 1877 the bound volume was sold to Mr. Pierce's sister, Mrs. Henry Keyes, and was inherited by the Keyes' children, Isabella and Henry Wilder Keyes.

Mr. Keyes was a United States senator from New Hampshire, and for many years he read Mr. Lincoln's address on the floor of the Senate to commemorate the Civil War President's birthday. Early in 1930 Mr. Keyes sold the manuscripts to a New York autograph dealer, Thomas F. Madigan, for $100,000. A short time later, James C. Ames, a Chicago investment banker, paid $150,000 for the volume. After the death of Mr. Ames in 1943, his widow had the manuscript appraised. The reported appraisal figure was $60,000.

The Illinois State Historical Library in Springfield was most anxious to acquire this manuscript. Chicago merchant Marshall Field donated $10,000 toward its purchase, and the school children of Illinois contributed $50,000 in nickels and dimes. Each year thousands of people gaze in awe at the manuscript now on display in Springfield, Illinois.

The fourth copy of the Address is known as the "Bancroft Copy." This was the one which was unsuitable for lithographing but had been requested as a memento by the historian George Bancroft. Many of Mr. Bancroft's papers were given to libraries after his death, but this particular manuscript was inherited by his grandson, Wilder D. Bancroft, a chemistry professor at Cornell University.

Professor Bancroft kept the manuscript in his home at Ithaca, New York, for a number of years. However, in 1929 he sold it to a New York dealer for $90,000. Several years later it was purchased by Mrs. Nicholas H. Noyes of Indianapolis, Indiana. In 1949 Mrs. Noyes added the Bancroft Copy to a collection of other Lincoln documents which her family had given to Cornell University. Today it is preserved between large sheets of clear plastic and is normally kept in a safe in the Cornell University Library's Department of Rare Books. For special exhibits, it is placed in a

Executive Mansion,

Washington, , 186 .

Four score and seven years ago our fathers brought forth, upon this continent, a new nation, conceived in liberty, and dedicated to the proposition that "all men are created equal"

Now we are engaged in a great civil war, testing whether that nation, or any nation so conceived, and so dedicated, can long endure. We are met on a great battle field of that war. We have come to dedicate a portion of it, as a final resting place for those who died here, that the nation might live. This we may, in all propriety do. But, in a larger sense, we can not dedicate—we can not consecrate—we can not hallow, this ground—The brave men, living and dead, who struggled here, have hallowed it, far above our poor power to add or detract. The world will little note, nor long remember what we say here; while it can never forget what they did here.

It is rather for us, the living, ~~to stand here~~, we here be dedica

THE NICOLAY COPY: *Also called the "First Draft," this manuscript is almost certainly the one Lincoln used when he delivered the address, but he did not follow the text exactly. A second page of this draft did not survive. Once the property of John G. Nicolay, Lincoln's private secretary, this draft passed into the hands of John Hay, U.S. Secretary of State and Lincoln's former assistant private secretary, after Nicolay's death in 1901. In 1916 Hay's children presented this copy to the Library of Congress.*

ted to the great task remaining before us—
that, from these honored dead we take increased devotion to that cause for which
they here, gave the last full measure of devotion—that we here highly resolve these
dead shall not have died in vain; that
the nation, shall have a new birth of freedom, and that government of the people by
the people for the people, shall not perish from the earth.

Four score and seven years ago our fathers brought forth, upon this continent, a new nation, conceived in Liberty, and dedicated to the proposition that all men are created equal.

Now we are engaged in a great civil war, testing whether that nation, or any nation, so conceived, and so dedicated, can long endure. We are met here on a great battle-field of that war. We ~~are~~ have come ~~met~~ to dedicate a portion of it as ~~the~~ a final resting place ~~of~~ for those who here gave their lives that that nation might live. It is altogether fitting and proper that we should do this.

But in a larger sense we can not dedicate— we can not consecrate— we can not hallow this ground. The brave men, living and dead, who struggled here, have consecrated it far above our poor power to add or detract. The world will little note, nor long remember, what we say here, but can never forget what they did here. It is for us, the living, rather to be dedicated here to the unfinished work which they have, thus far, so nobly carried on. It is rather for us to be here dedicated to the great task remaining before us—that from these honored dead we take increased devotion to ~~the~~ that cause for which they here gave the last full measure of devotion—that we here highly resolve that these dead shall not have died in vain; that this nation shall have a new birth of freedom, and that this government of the people, by the people, for the people, shall not perish from the earth.

THE HAY COPY: *Also called the "Second Draft," this was Lincoln's first revision of the Gettysburg Address. Evidence suggests that the copy was made shortly after Lincoln's return to Washington and in compliance with a request for the original manuscript by David Wills, his Gettysburg host. John Hay was given the copy instead. Hay's children presented it, along with the "First Draft," to the Library of Congress in 1916.*

Four score and seven years ago our fathers brought forth upon this continent, a new nation, conceived in Liberty, and dedicated to the proposition that all men are created equal.

Now we are engaged in a great civil war, testing whether that nation, or any nation so conceived, and so dedicated, can long endure. We are met on a great battle-field of that war. We have come to dedicate a portion of that field, as a final resting place for those who here gave their lives, that that nation might live. It is altogether fitting and proper that we should do this.

But, in a larger sense, we can not dedicate — we can not consecrate — we can not hallow — this ground. The brave men, living and dead, who struggled here, have consecrated it, far above our poor power to add or detract. The world will little note, nor long remember, what we say here, but it can never forget what they did here. It is for us the living, rather, to be dedicated here to the unfinished work which they who fought here, have, thus far, so nobly advanced. It is rather for us to be here dedicated to the great task remaining before

THE EVERETT COPY: *It is not certain whether Lincoln made this copy, in which the words "under God" appear for the first time, before or after the request of Edward Everett and Mrs. Hamilton Fish, who wanted it as a donation to New York's Metropolitan Fair, April, 1864. Everett had the manuscript bound with his own*

us— that from these honored dead we take increased devotion to that cause for which they here gave
the last full measure of devotion— that we here
highly resolve that these dead shall not have
died in vain— that this nation, under God,
shall have a new birth of freedom— and that
government of the people, by the people, for the
people, shall not perish from the earth.

Gettysburg oration, but there is no record that the volume was ever sold at the Fair. The manuscript passed through a number of hands before it was purchased in 1944 with funds donated by the school children of Illinois and became the property of that State. It is kept in the Illinois State Historical Library at Springfield.

Four score and seven years ago our fathers brought forth, on this continent, a new nation, conceived in Liberty, and dedicated to the proposition that all men are created equal.

Now we are engaged in a great civil war, testing whether that nation, or any nation so conceived, and so dedicated, can long endure. We are met on a great battle-field of that war. We have come to dedicate a portion of that field, as a final resting-place for those who here gave their lives, that that nation might live. It is altogether fitting and proper that we should do this.

But, in a larger sense, we can not dedicate— we can not consecrate— we can not hallow— this ground. The brave men, living and dead, who struggled here, have consecrated it far above our poor power to add or detract. The world will little note, nor long remember what we say here, but it can never forget what they did here. It is for us the living, rather, to be dedicated here to the unfinished work which they who fought here have thus far so nobly advanced. It is rather for us to be here dedicated to the great task remaining be-

THE BANCROFT COPY: *Lincoln made this copy in February, 1864, at the request of historian George Bancroft on behalf of his step-son, Colonel Alexander Bliss. Colonel Bliss was collecting manuscripts for a volume,* Autograph Leaves of our Country's Authors, *which would be sold for the benefit of the Baltimore Sanitary Fair. This copy and the Everett Copy were mailed on the same day and*

fore us—that from these honored dead we take in-creased devotion to that cause for which they here gave the last full measure of devotion—that we here high-ly resolve that these dead shall not have died in vain—that this nation, under God, shall have a new birth of freedom—and that government of the people, by the people, for the people, shall not perish from the earth.

differed, aside from minor changes in punctuation, only in the use of "upon" and "on" in the first sentence. Bancroft's family sold it in 1929 to a New York dealer who later sold it to Mrs. Nicolas H. Noyes. She presented it in 1949 to the library of Cornell University at Ithaca, New York.

Address delivered at the dedication of the Cemetery at Gettysburg.

Four score and seven years ago our fathers brought forth on this continent, a new nation, conceived in Liberty, and dedicated to the proposition that all men are created equal.

Now we are engaged in a great civil war, testing whether that nation, or any nation so conceived and so dedicated, can long endure. We are met on a great battle-field of that war. We have come to dedicate a portion of that field, as a final resting place for those who here gave their lives, that that nation might live. It is altogether fitting and proper that we should do this.

But, in a larger sense, we can not dedi-

THE BLISS COPY: *John P. Kennedy, editor of* Autograph Leaves of Our Country's Authors, *felt that the Bancroft copy was not suitable for inclusion in the volume of facsimiles—it lacked margins and needed a heading and a signature. Lincoln made another copy complying with all of Kennedy's requests. This copy, which represents Lincoln's last known revision and is the only signed*

6

cate — we can not consecrate — we can not hallow — this ground. The brave men, living and dead, who struggled here, have consecrated it, far above our poor power to add or detract. The world will little note, nor long remember what we say here, but it can never forget what they did here. It is for us the living, rather, to be dedicated here to the unfinished work which they who fought here have thus far so nobly advanced. It is rather for us to be here dedicated to the great task remaining before us — that from these honored dead we take increased devotion to that cause for which they gave the last full measure of devotion — that we here highly resolve that these dead shall not have died in vain — that this nation, under God, shall have a new birth of freedom — and that government of the people,

and dated copy, has become accepted as the standard text. It remained in the Bliss family until 1949 when it was purchased by Oscar B. Cintas, who had once served as Cuban ambassador to the United States. In his will, Mr. Cintas left the copy to the people of the United States, and at his stipulation, it is now installed in the Lincoln Room in the White House.

by the people, for the people, shall not perish from the earth.

Abraham Lincoln.

November 19. 1863.

large case at the entrance to the Rare Books Department. The Library has insured this valuable piece of property for $100,000.

The last copy of the Gettysburg Address which Mr. Lincoln is known to have made is identified as the "Bliss Copy." This was the one which was to be used in the book published for the benefit of the Baltimore Sanitary Fair. This copy remained in the Bliss family for many years. However, in 1949 it was put up for auction at the Parke-Bernet Galleries in New York City.

A Cuban businessman, Oscar B. Cintas, paid $54,000 for the Bliss Copy. Mr. Cintas had formerly been an ambassador to the United States and had become very much interested in Lincoln lore. He displayed the Bliss Copy in the library of his Havana home. Whenever a visitor entered, the door was always locked behind him; armed guards were on duty around the clock. After Mr. Cintas died, the executors of his will discovered that he wished to give the Bliss Copy to the White House so that it might be displayed in the Lincoln Room. A special messenger took the Bliss Copy in a blue leather case to the White House, and it was presented to President Eisenhower with appropriate ceremony in 1959. Today it is in the Lincoln Room, just as the former ambassador wished.

It is interesting to note that the First Draft contains 239 words while the Bliss Copy has 272 words. It is probable that in making his revision, President Lincoln checked over the Associated Press reports of his speech and found that he had said a few more words, extemporaneously, than he had actually written on his original manuscript.

Whatever the reason for the added words, historians believe that it is this final copy which Mr. Lincoln hoped would be remembered as his Gettysburg Address. Therefore, it is the Bliss Copy that has become the standard and authentic version of what President Lincoln said on November 19, 1863, when dedicating the National Cemetery at Gettysburg, Pennsylvania.

TEN

The World Has Long Remembered

MORE than one hundred years have elapsed since Mr. Lincoln delivered his "few appropriate remarks." The fame of the Gettysburg Address has become world-wide. Translated into almost every language, the speech ranks high in the world of fine literature.

In its final form the Gettysburg Address contains only ten sentences and a total of 272 words. They are plain, simple words—"the little fellers," Mr. Lincoln liked to call them. Analysis shows that 204 of the words have only one syllable, 50 have two, and *only* 18 have three or more syllables. Certainly it was the work of a genius.

Perhaps the simplicity of his writing is best explained by citing a conversation Mr. Lincoln once had with the Rev. John Gulliver. After Mr. Lincoln's famous Cooper Union

Address which was delivered in New York City, in February, 1860, the Rev. Gulliver asked Mr. Lincoln how he was able to express himself with such simplicity.

Mr. Lincoln explained that as a very small child he would become angry when anyone spoke to him in a way that he could not understand. Further, he said, "I could not sleep . . . when I got on such a hunt for an idea until I had caught it; and when I thought I had got it, I was not satisfied until I had repeated it over and over; until I had put it in language plain enough, as I thought, for any boy I knew to comprehend. This was a kind of passion with me and has stuck by me; for I am never easy now, when I am handling a thought, till I have bounded it north and bounded it south, and bounded it east and bounded it west."

In the early days of his political career, Mr. Lincoln did not speak to large audiences. At first he would talk with only two or three who were working in the fields, then perhaps to ten or twelve men gathered in a schoolhouse or a store. In these little speeches he always attempted to say things that even the least intelligent in his limited audience could understand.

Evidence of this meticulous preoccupation with words is revealed in all the writing Mr. Lincoln did after he became President. He rarely made an impromptu speech. Everything he said in public was prepared with great care. While he was writing out speeches or documents, the President often pronounced words or sentences aloud before putting them on paper. His many writings still in existence reveal that he was persistent in revising and editing what he had written.

Critics of fine literature have called the Gettysburg Ad-

White House Collection

The Bliss Copy of the Gettysburg Address, now on permanent display in the Lincoln bedroom of the White House.

dress "the only great prose poem of classical perfection in modern English." At Oxford University in England it is studied as "a perfect speciman of English composition." Countless students of American history are asked to memorize Mr. Lincoln's speech. In the light of its memorable background, let's examine the address for a clearer understanding of what was expressed.

> FOURSCORE AND SEVEN YEARS AGO OUR FATHERS BROUGHT FORTH ON THIS CONTINENT, A NEW NATION, CONCEIVED IN LIBERTY, AND DEDICATED TO THE PROPOSITION THAT ALL MEN ARE CREATED EQUAL.

In this opening sentence, President Lincoln sets the stage for his remarks, carrying his audience back to July 4, 1776, when the Declaration of Independence was adopted. Historians often point out that Mr. Lincoln first referred to the founding fathers in an impromptu speech which he was called upon to make on the evening of July 7 from an upstairs window of the White House. News of the great victory at Gettysburg had reached Washington and a procession, headed by a brass band, had formed and marched to the Executive Mansion to cheer Mr. Lincoln. When he stepped to the window to address the crowd, he said, "Eighty-odd years since, on the fourth of July, for the first time in the history of the world, a nation, by its representatives assembled, declared as a self-evident truth that all men are created equal." In the excitement of the moment, the President did not trust his subtraction, using the expression "eighty-odd." But before writing the Gettysburg Address, he had taken time to compute the years accurately.

The poetic beauty of Mr. Lincoln's writing is shown in his very first words, "Fourscore and seven." How much more rhythmical this is than merely saying, "Eighty-seven . . ." There is also an interesting implication in the phrase, ". . . dedicated to the proposition . . ." Those who have analyzed the address believe that this phrase was a direct result of Mr. Lincoln's study of the mathematician Euclid. As a young congressman, he studied "and nearly mastered" the six books of Euclid. Had he not done this, it is probable that this phrase would not have occurred to Mr. Lincoln.

NOW WE ARE ENGAGED IN A GREAT CIVIL WAR, TESTING WHETHER THAT NATION, OR ANY NATION SO CONCEIVED AND SO DEDICATED, CAN LONG ENDURE.

When the Civil War began there was much confusion about the issues which were at stake. Secretary of State Seward wanted a foreign war which would divert attention from the confusion in our country. The New York editor, Horace Greeley, advocated that the seceding states be allowed to go their own way. In the midst of all this confusion, Mr. Lincoln said, "I see my duty before me as plain as a turnpike road." In his mind there was never any question about which way the country should be led. At the National Cemetery dedication, the President brought his audience up to the present with the words, "Now we are engaged in a great Civil War." Yet it is notable that there

The Lane Studio, Gettysburg, Pa.

The Lincoln Address Memorial in the National Cemetery at Gettysburg.

is no hatred, no bitterness toward the South in his statement.

Inspiration for the phrase ". . .testing whether that nation, or any nation so conceived and so dedicated, can long endure. . ." may have come from a conversation with William Evans, the English liberal. Mr. Evans had called at the White House the day after the President had answered Mr. Wills' invitation to speak at Gettysburg. The Englishman had come to America to have a firsthand view of what he called this "experiment in democracy." All the world was watching the American Civil War, Mr. Evans had said, waiting to see whether democracy would actually work.

WE ARE MET ON A GREAT BATTLEFIELD OF THAT WAR. WE HAVE COME TO DEDICATE A PORTION OF THAT FIELD, AS A FINAL RESTING PLACE FOR THOSE WHO HERE GAVE THEIR LIVES THAT THAT NATION MIGHT LIVE. IT IS ALTOGETHER FITTING AND PROPER THAT WE SHOULD DO THIS.

Mr. Lincoln had been asked to dedicate the cemetery. Here, in these three sentences, he has actually done what he was invited to do, choosing his words with great deliberation, putting them together in such a way as to comfort the people who had lost sons or brothers or fathers in this great battle.

BUT, IN A LARGER SENSE, WE CAN NOT DEDICATE—WE CAN NOT CONSECRATE—WE CAN

NOT HALLOW—THIS GROUND. THE BRAVE MEN, LIVING AND DEAD, WHO STRUGGLED HERE, HAVE CONSECRATED IT, FAR ABOVE OUR POOR POWER TO ADD OR DETRACT.

As Commander-in-chief, Mr. Lincoln felt a deep responsibility for the men he had to send into battle. He never flinched from issuing combat orders, yet his all-encompassing sympathy reached out to every soldier and his family. In these two sentences he pays a beautiful and sincere tribute to all fighting men, both North and South.

Mr. Lincoln took the simple verb "can not," and by repeating it three times, gave it rhythmical cadence in combination with the words "dedicate," "consecrate," and "hallow." Again there is a touch of the poet in the President's writing.

The manuscript of the First Draft reads, ". . .our poor power to add or detract." However, newsmen at the dedication reported that Mr. Lincoln said, ". . .our power to add or detract," leaving out the word "poor." But the four copies made after the Address was delivered all contain the word "poor," so that it is quite evident Mr. Lincoln wanted to include the word which he inadvertently left out during his delivery.

THE WORLD WILL LITTLE NOTE, NOR LONG REMEMBER WHAT WE SAY HERE, BUT IT CAN NEVER FORGET WHAT THEY DID HERE.

Part of the greatness of Mr. Lincoln's character lies in

his utter humility. His lack of pretense, his pride in his humble beginnings has endeared him to successive generations of Americans. It is interesting to note that in the entire Gettysburg Address, the pronoun "I" is never used. Not many chief executives would have been so modest.

Mr. Lincoln was never convinced that he had anything worthwhile to say, or that he said it in any but the most ordinary fashion. On that November 19, the President truly believed that his words were unimportant. History has proven otherwise.

IT IS FOR US THE LIVING, RATHER, TO BE DEDICATED HERE TO THE UNFINISHED WORK WHICH THEY WHO FOUGHT HERE HAVE THUS FAR SO NOBLY ADVANCED.

Now Mr. Lincoln begins his challenge not only to his listening audience, but to the country at large. Here he gives a reason, a meaning for the continuance of the Civil War.

IT IS RATHER FOR US TO BE HERE DEDICATED TO THE GREAT TASK REMAINING BEFORE US —THAT FROM THESE HONORED DEAD WE TAKE INCREASED DEVOTION TO THAT CAUSE FOR WHICH THEY GAVE THE LAST FULL MEASURE OF DEVOTION—THAT WE HERE HIGHLY RESOLVE THAT THESE DEAD SHALL NOT HAVE DIED IN VAIN—THAT THIS NATION, UNDER GOD, SHALL HAVE A NEW BIRTH OF FREEDOM—AND THAT GOVERNMENT OF THE

PEOPLE, BY THE PEOPLE, FOR THE PEOPLE, SHALL NOT PERISH FROM THE EARTH.

In preparing the Gettysburg Address Mr. Lincoln had written ". . .that this nation shall have a new birth of freedom. . ." Historians believe that in the solemnity of the hour, Mr. Lincoln added the words "under God" to emphasize that the country must rely on the power of a Divine Being. In all the copies which were made later in Washington, the words "under God" are included.

These few simple words—words that were deeply felt and carefully chosen—have as great a challenge today as they did on that faraway November afternoon in 1863. The world *has* long remembered what Mr. Lincoln said at Gettysburg. The ideals which he expressed so eloquently have become a way of life for the American people and the freedom-loving nations of the world.

Bibliography

ANGLE, PAUL MCCLELLAND (editor). *The Lincoln Reader.* New Brunswick: Rutgers University Press, 1947.

ANGLE, PAUL MCCLELLAND and EARL SCHENCK MIERS (editors). *The Living Lincoln: His Mind, His Times, and the War He Fought. Reconstructed from His Own Writings.* New Brunswick: Rutgers University Press, 1955.

ANGLE, PAUL MCCLELLAND (compiler). *New Letters and Papers of Lincoln.* Boston: Houghton, Mifflin, 1930.

BARTON, WILLIAM ELEAZAR. *Lincoln at Gettysburg.* Indianapolis: The Bobbs-Merrill Company, 1930.

BROOKS, NOAH. *Washington in Lincoln's Time.* New York: The Century Company, 1895.

BRYAN, GEORGE SANDS. *The Great American Myth.* New York: Carrick and Evans, Inc., 1940.

BULLARD, FREDERICK. *Lincoln in Marble and Bronze.* New Brunswick: Rutgers University Press, 1952.

CARMICHAEL, ORTON H. *Lincoln's Gettysburg Address.* New York: Abingdon Press, 1917.

CARR, CLARK. *Lincoln at Gettysburg.* Chicago: Lakeside Press, 1906.

CATTON, BRUCE. A *Stillness at Appomattox.* New York: Doubleday & Company, 1953.

CHARNWOOD, GODFREY RATHBONE BENSON, LORD. *Abraham Lincoln.* Garden City, New York: Garden City Publishing Company, 1917.

CROOK, WILLIAM H. *Memories of the White House: The Home Life of our Presidents from Lincoln to Roosevelt.* Boston: Little, Brown & Company, 1911.

CUTHBERT, NORMA BARRETT. *Lincoln and the Baltimore*

Plot: From Pinkerton Records and Related Papers. San Marino, California: The Huntington Library, 1949.

DAUGHERTY, JAMES. *Abraham Lincoln.* New York: Viking Press, 1943.

FROTHINGHAM, PAUL R. *Edward Everett, Orator and Statesman.* Boston: Houghton, Mifflin, 1925.

HERTZ, EMANUEL (editor). *Lincoln Talks: A Biography in Anecdote.* New York: The Viking Press, 1939.

HUNGERFORD, EDWARD. *The Story of the Baltimore and Ohio Railroad.* Volumes I, II. New York: G. P. Putnam's Sons, 1928.

KRANZ, HENRY B. (editor). *Abraham Lincoln, A New Portrait.* New York: G. P. Putnam's Sons, 1959.

LEECH, MARGARET. *Reveille in Washington, 1860-1865.* Garden City, New York: Garden City Publishing Co., Inc., 1941.

LINCOLN, ABRAHAM. *The Collected Works of Abraham Lincoln.* Roy P. Basler (editor); Marion Dolores Pratt and Lloyd A. Dunlap (assistant editors). 9 volumes. New Brunswick: Rutgers University Press, 1953-55.

LORANT, STEFAN. *Lincoln: A Picture Story of his Life.* New York: Harper & Brothers, 1957.

MEARNS, DAVID C. *Largely Lincoln.* New York: St. Martin's Press, 1961.

MEARNS, DAVID C. and DUNLAP, LLOYD A. *Long Remembered: Notes on the Preparation of the Address.* Washington, D. C.: Library of Congress, 1963.

MESERVE, FREDERICK H. *The Photographs of Abraham Lincoln.* New York: Harcourt, Brace, 1944.

MITGANG, HERBERT (editor). *Lincoln: As They Saw Him.* New York: Rinehart & Company, 1956.

MONAGHAN, JAY. *Diplomat in Carpet Slippers: Abraham*

Lincoln Deals with Foreign Affairs. Indianapolis: Bobbs-Merrill Company, 1945.

NEVINS, ALLAN (editor). *Lincoln and the Gettysburg Address:* Commemorative Papers. Urbana, Illinois: The University of Illinois Press, 1964.

NEWMAN, RALPH G. (editor). *Lincoln for the Ages*. Garden City, New York: Doubleday & Company, Inc., 1960.

POTTER, JOHN MASON. *Thirteen Desperate Days*. New York: Ivan Obolensky, 1964.

QUARLES, BENJAMIN. *Lincoln and the Negro*. New York: Oxford University Press, 1962.

RANDALL, JAMES G. *Mr. Lincoln*. One-volume edition, Richard N. Current (editor). New York: Dodd, Mead & Company, 1957.

RANDALL, RUTH P. *Mary Lincoln: Biography of a Marriage*. Boston: Little, Brown and Company, 1953.

RANDALL, RUTH P. *Lincoln's Sons*. Boston: Little, Brown and Company, 1955.

SANDBURG, CARL. *Abraham Lincoln: The Prairie Years, The War Years*. 6 volumes. New York: Harcourt, Brace & Company, 1926-39.

SANDBURG, CARL and ANGLE, PAUL MCCLELLAND. *Mary Lincoln: Wife and Widow*. New York: Harcourt, Brace & Company, 1932.

STARR, JOHN W. *Lincoln and the Railroads*. New York: Dodd, Mead & Company, 1927.

THOMAS, BENJAMIN P. *Abraham Lincoln: A Biography*. New York: Alfred A. Knopf, 1952.

WEAVER, JOHN D. *Tad Lincoln: Mischief-Maker in the White House*. New York: Dodd, Mead & Company, 1963.

WEIK, JESSE W. *The Real Lincoln*. Boston: Houghton, Mifflin Company, 1922.

Index

About the Author

Mary Kay Phelan was born and raised in Baldwin City, Kansas. She received her A.B. degree from DePauw University and her A.M. degree from Northwestern University. *Mr. Lincoln Speaks At Gettysburg* reflects her great interest in writing books that will bring American history alive and make it meaningful for today's young people.

Mrs. Phelan's other books are: *The White House, The Circus,* and *Mother's Day*. She lives in Davenport, Iowa, with her husband and two sons.